GREAT MYSTERIES

Astrology

OPPOSING VIEWPOINTS®

Look for these and other exciting *Great Mysteries: Opposing Viewpoints* books:

GREAT MYSTERIES

Astrology

OPPOSING VIEWPOINTS®

by Mary-Paige Royer

Greenhaven Press, Inc.   P.O. Box 289009, San Diego, California 92198-0009

Library of Congress Cataloging-in-Publication Data

Royer, Mary-Paige
    Astrology : opposing viewpoints / by Mary-Paige Royer
       p. cm. — (Great mysteries)
    Includes bibliographical references and index.
    Summary: Discusses the history and uses of astrology and presents opposing viewpoints on its validity.
    ISBN 0-89908-090-1
    1. Astrology—Juvenile literature. [1. Astrology.] I. Title. II. Series: Great Mysteries.
BF1708 . 1 . R65   1991
133.5—dc20   91-21657

Acknowledgments

The author wishes to acknowledge the kind contributions of the following people: *Astronomers* Andrew Fraknoi, Executive Officer of the Astronomical Society of the Pacific; Professor James Kaler, University of Illinois; Professor Harry Shipman, University of Delaware; *Astrologers* Karen Anderson, Northern Star Astrology; Mary Downing, Secretary, National Council for GeoCosmic Research; Marion March, Aquarious Workshops; Joan Negus, Director of Education, National Council for GeoCosmic Research; Shirley Strasburg, Minneapolis, MN. These professionals provided much helpful information and advice. Any errors in interpretation are the author's.

Contents

Introduction

This book is written for the curious—those who want to explore the mysteries that are everywhere. To be human is to be constantly surrounded by wonderment. How do birds fly? Are ghosts real? Can animals and people communicate? Was King Arthur a real person or a myth? Why did Amelia Earhart disappear? Did history really happen the way we think it did? Where did the world come from? Where is it going?

Great Mysteries: Opposing Viewpoints books are intended to offer the reader an opportunity to explore some of the many mysteries that both trouble and intrigue us. For the span of each book, we want the reader to feel that he or she is a scientist investigating the extinction of the dinosaurs, an archaeologist searching for clues to the origin of the great Egyptian pyramids, a psychic detective testing the existence of ESP.

One thing all mysteries have in common is that there is no ready answer. Often there are *many* answers but none on which even the majority of authorities agrees. *Great Mysteries: Opposing Viewpoints* books introduce the intriguing views of the experts, allowing the reader to participate in their explorations, their theories, and their disagreements as they try to explain the mysteries of our world.

But most readers won't want to stop here. These *Great Mysteries: Opposing Viewpoints* aim to stimulate the reader's curiosity. Although truth is often impossible to discover, the search is fascinating. It is up to the reader to examine the evidence, to decide whether the answer is there—or to explore further.

"Penetrating so many secrets, we cease to believe in the unknowable. But there it sits nevertheless, calmly licking its chops."

H.L. Mencken, American essayist

Prologue

Predictions for Presidents

Nancy Reagan will never forget the terror of March 30, 1981. On that day, John Hinckley tried to assassinate her husband, then-president Ronald Reagan. In the aftermath of this near tragedy, Nancy Reagan feared that someone would try to harm her husband again. "I'm scared every time he leaves the house and I don't think I breathe until he gets home," she said in her memoirs, *My Turn*. "I cringe every time we step out of a car or leave a building."

Advice from the Stars

Shortly after the assassination attempt, Nancy Reagan learned that an astrologer named Joan Quigley had predicted that March 31 would be a bad day for the president. Mrs. Reagan quickly called this astrologer on the phone and told her about her fears for her husband's safety. This was the first of many calls between the First Lady and the astrologer. The two began to talk frequently, becoming friends. Twice a month, Mrs. Reagan would ask the astrologer which dates were safe and which were dangerous for the president to appear in public.

Mrs. Reagan tried to keep her conversations with Quigley as private as possible. In her memoirs she said that if her contact with an astrologer came out, "It could prove embarrassing to Ronnie." But Mrs.

(opposite page) Second-century A.D. Egyptian astronomer Ptolemy (left) and Greek philosopher Pythagoras study an astrology book in this medieval engraving.

Reagan often spoke to then-chief-of-staff Donald Regan about altering the president's schedule based on the astrologer's predictions. Regan said he began color coding his desk calendar to keep track of good, bad, and "iffy" days for the president. Important dates like the 1985 Geneva summit meeting with the USSR's president Gorbachev had to be cleared with the astrologer, he says.

Seeking Wisdom

Joan Quigley was not the first astrologer consulted by the Reagans. In fact, they once consulted with astrologer Jeanne Dixon, and both read the column of astrologer Sydney Omarr daily in the *Washington Post*. The Reagans also sought the advice of astrologer Carroll Righter in their early acting days in Hollywood in the 1940s when astrology was considered quite fashionable. Many suspect that astrology was the reason the president changed the time of his first inauguration as governor of California from midnight to 12:10 A.M. over a decade ago. And some astrologers believe that Reagan picked his unusual inauguration time as president—after 1:00 A.M.—based on astrology.

Soviet foreign minister Eduard Shevardnadze, Soviet president Mikhail Gorbachev, U.S. president Ronald Reagan, and U.S. secretary of state George Shultz (left to right) shake hands at the close of the 1985 summit meeting in Geneva, Switzerland, as other officials look on. According to White House sources, the Reagans consulted an astrologer when scheduling important events like the summit meeting.

The Reagans belong to a long tradition of leaders who seek wisdom and advice from the stars. Monarchs ranging from Catherine de Medici to King Arthur to Edward III of England kept astrologers close at hand. A quotation attributed to Aristotle shows how heavily some leaders relied upon astrology, even for the least important activities: "O most clement king, if it is at all possible, you should neither rise up nor sit down nor eat nor drink nor do anything without the advice of men learned in the art of astrology."

Many court astrologers predicted events ranging from when someone of importance was going to die to what was the right moment to enter a battle and overthrow the enemy. But the astrologer's main function was to tell royal clients, "in an acceptable form, what they already believed, or wanted to hear," writes Hilary M. Carey in an essay called "Astrology at the English Court in the Later Middle Ages." Carey says, "It is not difficult to understand why . . . rulers have been so attracted to astrology, as to any system which claimed to predict the future, avert disaster and hasten the overthrow of the enemy."

In the modern age, few people fret about how to overthrow their enemy. But to people through the ages, monarch or not, astrology's promise of predicting the future was—and still is—part of its appeal.

"There is not even a blade of grass, however infinitesimal, that is not ruled by some star."

Thirteenth-century rabbi Eleazar, *Zohar*

"Our remedies in ourselves do lie, which we ascribe to heaven."

Sixteenth-century playwright William Shakespeare, *All's Well That Ends Well*

One

What Is Astrology?

The astrologer sits at her desk and slips a floppy disc into her computer. The computer loads her astrological software program. As the first screen blinks on, the astrologer types in the following information: 10:05 P.M.; Chicago; latitude, forty-one degrees north, fifty-one minutes; longitude, eighty-seven degrees west, thirty-nine minutes; April 4, 1976. Three minutes later, the computer spits out a mysterious-looking diagram. It looks like a sundial crisscrossed into twelve sections, with a smaller circle in its center. Curious, primitive symbols, like hieroglyphs, are sprinkled about the sundial.

Plenty of Potential Customers

This is a modern-day astrologer on the job, compiling someone's horoscope, a map of the stars on the day her client was born. Our astrologer is one of roughly ten thousand that practice astrology in the United States today. And they have plenty of potential customers, since approximately forty million people in the United States—about one in three—are interested in astrology. These people run the gamut from stockbrokers to students, from celebrities to corporate executives.

How can astrology attract the interest of such a wide range of people? Derek and Julia Parker,

(opposite page) A copper engraving depicts the twelve signs of the zodiac.

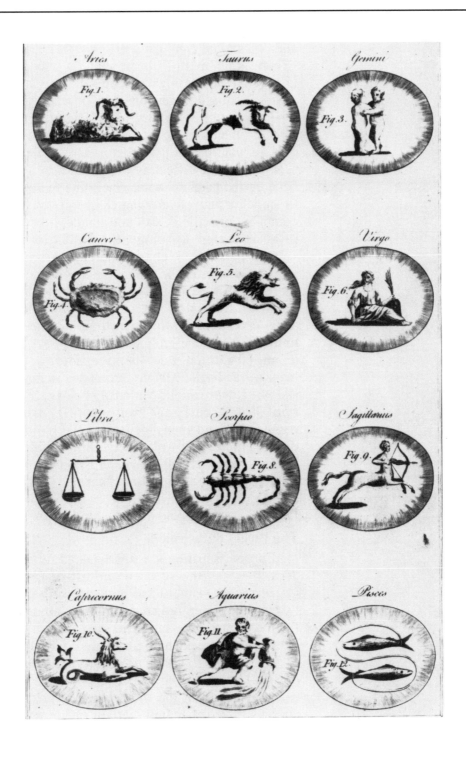

authors of *The New Compleat Astrologer*, answer, "There is no area of life in which a good working knowledge of astrology is not useful, and in which a professional astrologer cannot be of practical help."

People use astrology to forecast the weather; foretell when someone is susceptible to illness and explain what parts of the body are most vulnerable; prophesy events affecting the welfare of a country, from earthquakes to wars; determine the best times to launch a new advertising campaign, buy another company, or trade stocks and bonds. Most popular of all is "natal" astrology, the casting of an individual's natal (birth) chart or horoscope.

Like phases of the moon, interest in astrology in the United States has waxed and waned over the centuries. But today, signs of astrology's popularity are everywhere. All major metropolitan newspapers in the United States contain a horoscope column, as do most women's and some general audience magazines. The telephone directories in many cities list dial-a-horoscope message services. Most bookstores carry a number of astrological magazines, and many general interest magazines devote articles to astrology. Astrology books written by well-known astrologers like Linda Goodman ring up strong sales. Goodman's publisher was so confident of the profitability of her second book, *Love Signs,* that it paid her $2.5 million for it.

The Basics of Astrology

English astrologer Rupert Gleadow describes astrology as "the science and art of describing persons and events of the past, present, and future by correctly interpreting maps of the sky drawn up for the appropriate moments and places." Astrologers study the changing patterns and movements of the planets, stars, sun, and moon in relation to the earth. They believe that the position of these celestial bodies at the moment of a person's birth endows him or her with certain characteristics. In

An engraving by seventeenth-century artist Jacob de Gheyn combines both the constellation and the sign of Pisces the Fish to show how the ancients saw the zodiac in the stars.

fact, they think that the heavenly bodies exert a lifelong influence on both people and events.

Much of what we know about astrology today has evolved from the observations made by ancient peoples. Centuries ago, people imagined they saw creatures and objects in the sky in constellations, or clusters of stars. "They fancied that certain groups of stars sketched the outlines of men or animals or other familiar objects, and they made up stories to explain how this or that hero or god or creature had done such great deeds here on earth that he had won immortality and was affixed forever in the night sky," writes Gary Jennings in *The Teenager's Realistic Guide to Astrology*.

As the ancients peered into the skies above, it appeared to them that the constellations and sun revolved around the earth. The early skygazers observed that the constellations shifted slightly from east to west each day. As some constellations gradually sank below the western horizon, new ones rose on the eastern horizon.

Over time, the ancients decided that some

De Gheyn's engravings of the zodiac signs Aries the Ram and Cancer the Crab as they appear within their constellations.

constellations were more important than others. Most important were the ones that traveled in the same path as the sun. Twelve of these later became astrological symbols. These twelve constellations seemed to form a circle, or band, in the sky. This band became known as the ecliptic because eclipses also take place upon this path, according to Leslie Fleming-Mitchell, author of *Astrology Terms*.

The twelve astrological constellations are called the zodiac, a name that comes from Greek words meaning "circle of animals." The twelve constellations that make up the zodiac are Aries the Ram, Taurus the Bull, Gemini the Twins, Cancer the Crab, Leo the Lion, Virgo the Virgin, Libra the Scales, Scorpio the Scorpion, Sagittarius the Archer, Capricorn the Goat, Aquarius the Water Bearer, and Pisces the Fish.

The Zodiac and the Year

Traditionally, people believed the sun passes through one sign of the zodiac approximately every thirty-day period. Thus, each of the twelve signs of the zodiac is said to correspond to one of the twelve months of the year. Many ancient societies considered the first day of spring, March 21, to be the first day of the year. This day, also called the vernal equinox, is thus the day the astrological calendar begins. In ancient times, when the sun began its round of the sky at this time every year, the most visible sign of the zodiac was Aries, in the easternmost segment of the circle. That is why it became the first sign of the zodiac. After Aries, the sun always passes through the other eleven signs of the zodiac in this order: Taurus, Gemini, Cancer, Leo, Virgo, Libra, Scorpio, Sagittarius, Capricorn, Aquarius, and finally, Pisces.

Everyone is born under a sun sign, that is, the zodiac constellation through which the sun passes at the moment of a person's birth. Those born on or very close to the day the sun sign changes are said

God and his angels rule over the universe depicted as a horoscope containing the signs, houses, and planets of the zodiac.

to be born on the cusp, or changing point. An astrologer may have to do very careful calculations to figure out which sun sign has the most influence on this person.

Astrologers believe the sun, as the center of the solar system, represents one's spirit, driving force, and inner sense of purpose, write Dodie and Allan Edmands in *The Children's Astrologer*. So, the particular character of a sun sign will influence one's personality. The sun sign also describes how a person expresses his or her core self. For example, if a woman's sun sign is Aries, she will express

"Nothing exists nor happens in the visible sky that is not sensed in some hidden moment by the faculties of Earth and Nature."

Sixteenth-century scientist Johannes Kepler, *De Stella Nova*

"Men at some time are masters of their fate. The fault, dear Brutus, is not in our stars, but in ourselves, that we are underlings."

Sixteenth-century playwright William Shakespeare, *Julius Caesar*

herself dynamically and impulsively; will be bright, eager, and active; and will be likely to look for novel ways to assert herself, write the Edmands. On the other hand, a woman whose sun sign is Taurus will be "more cautious in self-expression, preferring [the] familiar and comfortable . . . to the exploration of uncharted territory."

Astrologers also consider the moon an important influence. In fact, the ancient Romans considered the moon sign to be more significant than the sun sign. A person's moon sign is the sign of the zodiac the moon was passing through at the time of his or her birth. (The moon passes through the twelve signs of the zodiac about every two-and-a-half days.) To astrologers, the moon represents a person's emotional response to life. It can tell an astrologer about a person's attitudes and likely reactions to others. For example, a man whose moon sign is Aries can have highly emotional and impulsive responses, write Frances Sakoian and Louis Acker in *The Astrologer's Handbook*. Highly independent, he may insist on following his own path of action, have a tendency to dominate others emotionally, and be prone to take the reactions of others personally, write the authors.

Appendix C lists the moon signs for birthdays between 1975 and 1984. Here is a brief description of the moon's influence, according to Gary Jennings:

If the moon is in	you are likely to be
Aries	quickly aroused; enthusiastic; hot-tempered; fiercely independent
Taurus	calm and relaxed; sentimental; possessive
Gemini	very changeable; witty and perceptive; impulsive
Cancer	gentle, passive, and shy, with occasional outbursts of enthusiasm

Leo	strongly emotional; passionate; attracted to good; well-organized
Virgo	precise; clean; a perfectionist; judgmental
Libra	well-balanced and moderate; private; a hider of feelings
Scorpio	intense and forceful; highly energetic; go to extremes
Sagittarius	eager; inquisitive; a born adventurer; keep feelings at a distance; guided by reason rather than emotion
Capricorn	dependable; committed; driven to succeed; withdrawn
Aquarius	warm and generous, friendly and tolerant, but extremely independent, leading you to have many acquaintances but few intimate friends
Pisces	repressive of your own emotions but a good empathizer with others; sympathetic; impressionable

Planetary Influence

The position of the planets also has an impact on people, say astrologers. The stars that make up the constellations of the zodiac are fixed in place, but the planets constantly move among the signs of the zodiac, forming different patterns. Astrologers have known since antiquity about five planets in our solar system—Mercury, Venus, Mars, Jupiter, and Saturn. The other three planets—Uranus, Neptune, and Pluto—were discovered in more recent times.

The ancients have long since ascribed certain personality traits to each planet. With its reddish tint, Mars made them think of bloodshed and so became the planet ruling war and violence. This fast-moving planet is said to represent aggres-

A diagram shows the planets of our solar system orbiting around the sun. As planets pass through the signs of the zodiac they blend the signs' characteristics with their own, according to astrologers. A person born with Mars in Aquarius, for example, has both Martian and Aquarian traits.

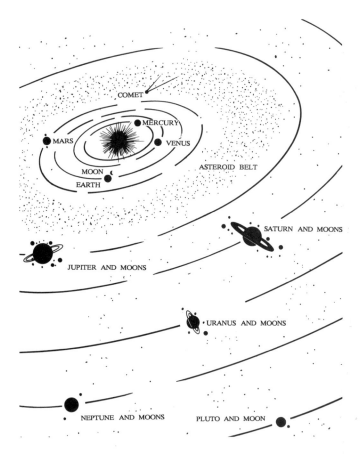

siveness and initiative. Slower-moving Jupiter has a friendly, fortunate aura. According to Marc Edmund Jones, author of *How to Learn Astrology*, the following qualities are associated with the planets:

sun	purpose	moon	feeling
Mars	initiative	Venus	acquisitiveness
Mercury	mentality	Jupiter	enthusiasm
Saturn	sensitivity	Uranus	independence
Neptune	obligation	Pluto	obsession

As a planet passes through a sign of the zodiac, it supposedly absorbs and combines the characteristics of this sign with its own. At birth, a person picks up the energy radiated by any planet passing through his or her zodiac constellation. Each planet rules, or strongly influences, one or two signs of the zodiac, say astrologers. In his book *Astrology*, Louis MacNeice quotes a Roman poet named Minilius who described this interrelation of planets and zodiac:

> No sign nor planet serves itself alone,
> Each blends the other's virtues with its own,
> Mixing their force, and interchanged they reign,
> Signs [with] planets bound, and planets [with] signs again.

An astrologer might say that someone is a typical Jupiterian or Martian, meaning that that person displays qualities associated with the planet, says MacNeice.

In the second century A.D., Greek astronomer Claudius Ptolemy decided that the sun ruled the constellation Leo, since the sun shone its brightest when in this constellation from July 23 to August 23. Because the moon circles the earth directly and closely, Ptolemy considered it to be the most important planet after the sun. He decided that the moon ruled the sign next to Leo, Cancer. The other signs and their ruling planets are Aries, ruled by Mars; Taurus by Venus; Gemini by Mercury; Virgo by Mercury; Libra by Venus; Scorpio by Pluto and Mars; Sagittarius by Jupiter; Capricorn by Saturn; Aquarius by Uranus and Saturn; and Pisces by Neptune. If Mars is found in Aries, then it will make a person not only more of an Aries type, but also more of a Mars type, writes MacNeice.

The Twelve Houses

To fit the pattern of twelve sun signs and twelve months, "Ptolemy found it convenient to imagine the sky circle of 360 degrees to be partitioned into [twelve equal] segments called houses," writes Roy A. Gallant, author of *Astrology: Sense or Nonsense?* According to astrologers, these 30-degree segments, or houses, each represent an area of life experience.

"I have found in my work that everything in nature influences everything else; so why shouldn't the stars influence man?"

John Burroughs, nineteenth-century American naturalist

"Arguments that have no basis in common sense are always hard to refute. And so it is with astrology."

English astronomer Patrick Moore

For example, the first house represents one's personality and physical structure. Although different astrologers have slightly different interpretations for the twelve houses, here is what they are typically said to represent:

first house	=	personality and physical appearance
second house	=	money and possessions
third house	=	relationships and communication
fourth house	=	home and family life
fifth house	=	romance, creativity, and leisure
sixth house	=	health and work
seventh house	=	marriage
eighth house	=	change, business, and law
ninth house	=	travel and education
tenth house	=	career and community
eleventh house	=	friends and social life
twelfth house	=	secrets

Each house can contain one or more planets, since planets move about. Astrologers say that the positions of the planets and signs of the zodiac in the celestial sphere (the sky) at the time of one's birth take on significance depending on their locations in the various houses. For example, having the carefree, broad-minded zodiac sign of Aquarius in the second house, which relates to money, can mean that one is apt to lend money easily. Someone with the moon, which rules emotion, in his or her eighth house, which governs divorces and wills, could be emotional when dealing with these things. For a more complete description of the effect of each house, see appendix A at the end of this book.

The most important house is the first house, the house of the ascendant—the sign of the zodiac that rises over the eastern horizon at the exact moment of birth. The first house sign influences one's

Egyptian astronomer-geographer Claudius Ptolemy's astrological works still influence astrology today.

physical characteristics, personality, and general mode of expression, says Leslie Fleming-Mitchell. The ascendant sign also indicates the first impression one makes on others and one's style of relating. Someone with a rising sign in Pisces, for instance, will seem dreamy and vulnerable and will project his or her character in a quiet, sensitive manner.

The ascendant sign can modify the influence of the sun sign. For example, a man born with a sun sign in Aries would have the qualities of impulsiveness and passion. If he had Virgo as his ascendant sign, he would be more down-to-earth

This sixteenth-century engraving by Albrecht Dürer depicts many of the constellations perceived in the heavens.

and analytical. A Virgo tends to finish the task at hand, while an Aries wants to start but not finish a project. So this person would have his impulsiveness diminished because of the effect of the ascendant sign.

Astrologers usually assign special significance also to the signs and planets in the fourth, seventh, and tenth houses. The fourth house, or nadir, is in the six o'clock position. The seventh house contains the descendant, the sign of the zodiac that was setting on the western horizon at the time of a person's birth. It is directly opposite the ascendant, in the three o'clock position. The tenth house, at twelve o'clock, is also known as the mid-heaven. It is the sign of the zodiac that was directly overhead at one's birth.

An astrologer is someone who draws up a map of the sky for a particular moment and then makes generalizations or forecasts about the event relating to that moment. These maps are also called charts or horoscopes. The most common type of horoscope is the natal chart, drawn for the moment of a person's birth, from which the astrologer makes generalizations and predictions about a person's life. The name *horoscope* is derived from the Greek word *horoscopos*, meaning "a look at the hour." It refers to the hour for which the sky map is drawn, the hour of one's birth, for example, or of a marriage, business transaction, battle, or other event.

The Path of the Sun

As a map, a horoscope represents the path the sun appears to follow through the sky, so it takes the form of a 360-degree circle. Astrologers divide this circle into twelve slices, as if it were a pie. They number each slice, or house. Then they place the twelve signs of the zodiac around the outside of the circle. Astrologers always begin with the sign of the zodiac determined to be on the ascendant, the first zodiac sign to appear on the eastern horizon at birth or at the time of the event to be analyzed. (For simplicity, we will talk about the natal chart, the most common type of horoscope.) On a horoscope, the eastern horizon is placed on the left side of the circle, in the position of nine o'clock. After labeling the ascendant, astrologers place the remaining signs of the zodiac in order, in a counterclockwise direction, according to their position at the time of the person's birth. Then they place symbols representing the positions of the sun, moon, and other planets in the appropriate houses.

Most astrologers cast individual horoscopes for a specific birthdate, time (to the minute, if possible), and geographic location (longitude and latitude of a person's birthplace). Most tables are based on midnight or noon in Greenwich, England, since this is the starting point for time zones around the world. To chart a horoscope, an astrologer must convert a birth time to sidereal time (or star time) in

"If astrologers are able to foretell the future, why don't they break the bank at the world's casinos?"

Andrew Fraknoi, astronomer and executive officer of the Astronomical Society of the Pacific

"An astrologer is not a magician. Anyone who tells you that they can predict any event in the future, who, in the manner of the old fairground gypsy, tells you you are going to meet a tall, dark, handsome stranger, marry him and have three children, is no true astrologer."

Derek and Julia Parker, *The New Compleat Astrologer*

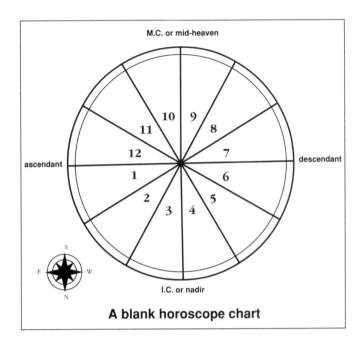

A blank horoscope chart

Greenwich. A reference book called an ephemeris tells the sidereal time for one's date of birth and the exact position of the moon, planets, and other celestial bodies in the universe on any given date. Astrologers use another reference book called a table of houses that tells how to determine which of the twelve zodiac signs are positioned on the house cusps.

Once the horoscope chart is complete, the astrologer interprets and summarizes the various influences of the celestial bodies. Most refer to a variety of reference materials for their interpretation. "The meanings of the various parts of the horoscope were settled long ago, and most astrologers accept them," says MacNeice.

A horoscope charted with all the necessary information is far more complex than are the overly simplified horoscopes published in newspapers that take only sun signs into account. Interpretation can be a complex process, requiring the "ability to grasp

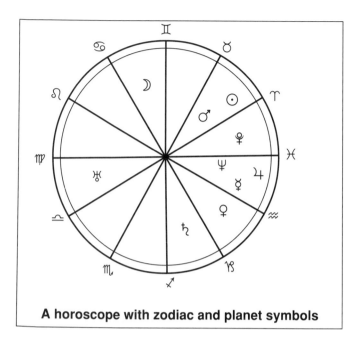

A horoscope with zodiac and planet symbols

and interpret all combinations and then, from the available evidence, to arrive at a reasonable synthesis of what it all means or is supposed to mean," writes MacNeice.

How the Stars Influence Life

So why do astrologers believe that the stars and planets influence our lives? Many of their beliefs grew out of theories of ancient civilizations. The ancients thought the earth was the center of the universe and all planets and stars revolved around it. They understood that the sun had a purpose—to warm the earth and help plants grow. Therefore, it seemed to them that other heavenly bodies had a purpose as well.

The ancients probably thought that the rays of light from celestial bodies contained "some kind of radiation or vibration working some sort of attraction like magnetism," writes author Gary Jennings. They reasoned that heavenly bodies had a gravitational force that, like magnetism, exerted a "pull on every

"If reading the stars has led astrologers to incorrect predictions nine times out of ten, they hardly seem like reliable guides to the uncertainties of life or the affairs of our country."

Andrew Fraknoi, astronomer and executive officer of the Astronomical Society of the Pacific

"The astrologer *cannot* predict every event. . . . An astrological aspect with regard to the future can correspond with any one of a variety of possibilities . . . yet the aspect still foretells the actual *trend* of circumstances."

Astrologer Jeff Mayo, *Astrology*

other body," including human beings. In other words, the ancients came to believe that heavenly bodies were "beaming some kind of force down onto the earth," writes Jennings.

Some astrologers talk about radiation when explaining the effect of the planets and stars. "The radiations emanating from the planets act as a stimulus on the tides, on vegetable and animal life, on the life beneath the surface of the seas, on the minerals beneath the surface of the earth, and on all that exists, grows, thrives, flourishes, subsists, endures, lives and breathes between heaven and earth," writes Beatrice Ryder in *Astrology: Your Personal Sun-Sign Guide*.

Astrologers point to many species of plants and animals that gear a variety of activities to phases of the moon. Sunspots, dark patches that flare up on the sun's surface, also seem to affect both humans and animals. One study indicated that mental patients in a hospital became more agitated and violent during occurrences of sunspots. Therefore, say astrologers, it is not unreasonable to assume that other planets also affect life on earth.

Skeptical Scientists

Today, most scientists, however, doubt that a strong connection exists between celestial occurrences and living organisms. Those scientists who acknowledge planetary influences on earth still do not see evidence that this validates astrology. "Astrology purports to believe that little points in the sky have magical powers and by some means influence life on earth," says Professor James Kaler, an astronomer at the University of Illinois. "This is absolute nonsense."

Most scientists say that astrology is based on folklore handed down by early people who did not understand what they saw in the sky. The typical skeptical scientist gives astrologers credit in only one area: Because ancient astrologers kept detailed

The ancients used many forms of divination to determine the course of events. Here, diviners tell a king's fortune from the liver of a sacrificed sheep.

records of the movement and positions of the celestial bodies, they laid the groundwork for astronomy. Beginning in 3000 B.C., the ancient Babylonian astrologers kept a careful watch on the skies. So did astrologers in many countries throughout the centuries.

The Oldest Science?

Many astrologers are fond of saying that astrology is the "oldest of all sciences," even though some would say it is more art than science. Astrologers can pluck endless examples of the central role astrology played in civilizations, particularly ancient ones. Why did ancient people gaze so intently into the skies? How was astrology interwoven into their lives?

Two

How Did Astrology Begin?

Since time immemorial, the allure of astrology has beckoned to civilizations around the globe. Ancient people craned their necks, scanning the night skies for clues to their fate and future in the position of the heavenly bodies. Through the centuries, astrology evolved from simple stargazing to a science and mystic art.

Astrology's origins can be traced at least as far back as 3000 B.C. Archaeologists have found clay tablets with astrological symbols on them at the ancient site of Babylon. The Babylonians connected what happened in the sky with events on earth. They thought heavenly bodies were omens of the gods that influenced everything from weather to the well-being of their country. H. J. Eysenck and D. K. B. Nias, in *Astrology: Science or Superstition?*, point out one example. Around 2470 B.C., they say, Babylonian astrologers determined that "if the moon can be seen the first night of the month, the country will be peaceful. . . . If the moon is surrounded by a halo, the king will reign supreme."

Religion and Cosmic Events

Ancient people gave particular attention to unusual events in the sky, like eclipses, comets, and meteor showers. Since these things were beyond the

(opposite page) An astronomer uses an astrolabe while one assistant takes notes and the other holds a reference book in this fourteenth-century illustration.

Ancient Babylonians worship
the sun god in this
eighteenth-century
engraving.

people's earthly knowledge, they looked for supernatural explanations. Unusual celestial events must
be messages from the gods, they thought. Roy A.
Gallant, author of *Astrology: Sense or Nonsense?*,
describes a Sumerian priest's ritual during a
frightening eclipse:

> The instant an eclipse began to take place, the
> priests . . . had to light a torch on the temple altar
> and recite chants to save the fields, rivers, and
> other parts of the land. Meanwhile, all the people
> had to cover their heads with their clothing and
> shout loudly, which always seemed to help restore

things to normal. Who could deny that such a ritual worked?

Obviously, it did, since the eclipse passed and the land was not harmed. So great was the people's fear of unusual events in the sky that few would be likely to have the courage to do nothing at all to find out just what would or would not happen.

Early astrologer-priests eventually began to associate certain constellations, zodiacal signs, and stars with gods. They also believed their king communicated with the gods to find out what the future held for their country. Kings relied heavily on astrologer-priests to help them interpret messages from the gods.

Many of these early astrologer-priests were astronomers as well. "As astronomers they studied the motions of the sun, moon, and the visible planets," writes Franklyn M. Branley in *The Age of Aquarius*. He continues, "As astrologers they read the skies for meanings, meanings that would affect the fate of the king and so the fate of the entire kingdom."

The science of astronomy gradually began to grow out of astrology, just as chemistry evolved from alchemy. The astrologers' careful records of such phenomena as the reappearance of certain comets were invaluable information for future astronomers, writes Gary Jennings. "The astrologers continued to find mystic messages in the skies without bothering much about the physical nature of the heavenly bodies they worked with," he says. But "astronomers began to scan the skies to learn just what the heavenly bodies were, how they were interrelated, and how their movements could be measured and explained."

The Greeks Adopt Astrology

After the Greeks conquered Babylon in 331 B.C., they adopted many of the Babylonians' beliefs about astrology. Over time, the Greeks developed

"No rational person would place any faith or reliance in a system based on the misconceptions of primitive people; a system built on a framework of pure invention, guesswork and oversimplified analogies; ignoring practically every scientific discovery that has been made; denying almost every astronomical theory that has been proved to be true, but which does not fit into astrology's traditional scheme of things."

Gary Jennings, *The Teenager's Realistic Guide to Astrology*

"No one should regard it as impossible that from the follies and blasphemies of astrologers may emerge a sound and useful body of knowledge."

Sixteenth-century scientist Johannes Kepler

astrology more than any other ancient civilization. These two civilizations—Babylon and Greece—used astrology in very different ways. The Babylonians primarily used astrology to predict the welfare of the state and king. The Greeks also used astrology in this way, but more importantly, they created horoscopes in the sixth century B.C., and they made astrology widely available to everyday people.

The Greeks also developed new ways to make horoscopes more individual. The Babylonians had considered only thirteen factors in a horoscope: the sun and the twelve signs of the zodiac. Since many people are born on the same day, many people would supposedly have the same horoscope reading. For example, states author Gary Jennings, approximately one-twelfth of the population is born with the sun in Taurus, since the sun is in Taurus for one month every year. This would assume that a vast population group would all exhibit similar Taurean qualities.

The Sky's Influence

The Greeks introduced more variation in horoscopes by making charts for a certain hour and minute, instead of for an entire month. And they introduced consideration of the ascendant, the constellation rising in the eastern sky at birth. The sun sign was important in determining a person's character, but one's ascendant sign could affect the impact of the sun sign, they decided.

Early people believed four elements comprised all things. They were fire, earth, air, and water. The Greeks assigned three signs of the zodiac to each of these elements. Aries, Sagittarius, and Leo were designated as fire signs; Cancer, Scorpio, and Pisces as water signs; Aquarius, Libra, and Gemini as air signs; and Taurus, Virgo, and Capricorn as earth signs.

Supposedly, these elements influence how well people get along with each other. People born under earth signs are said to be practical and energetic with strong personalities. Those born under air signs tend to be intellectual people interested in the arts and sciences, who express themselves well in speech and writing, writes Elinor Lander Horwitz in *The Soothsayer's Handbook: A Guide to Bad Signs and Good Vibrations*. Those born under fire signs possess ambition and courage, and those born under water signs are emotional, daydreaming people who are likely to be impractical, adds Horwitz.

People born under the earth signs are said to be compatible with the water signs. But people born under water signs—emotional and often impractical—will not mesh as well with the air signs. People born under air signs get along fine with fire signs. And the three signs of the same element all mix well with each other.

The Greeks also assigned the signs of the zodiac to parts of the body. Working from head to toe, they assigned the first sign, Aries, the head, and the last sign, Pisces, the feet. Supposedly, the stars in the zodiac signs influenced the body's parts and thus affected a person's health. Therefore, some people turned to astrologers for information and advice about health. They regarded astrologers as doctors who could treat diseases based on what they read in the charts of people visiting them, writes Leonard Everett Fisher in *Star Signs*.

Astrology and Physical Traits

Early astrologers even associated physical characteristics with the signs of the zodiac, writes Horwitz. For example, people with the sun sign Pisces were said to be short and rather fleshy, with pale soft skin and silky thin hair. They were likely to be graceful in movement with dimples and well-shaped hands and feet. Those born under the sun sign Libra tend to be tall and shapely with brown or black hair and good complexion, said early astrologers. Librans were also thought to have pleasant voices, writes Horwitz.

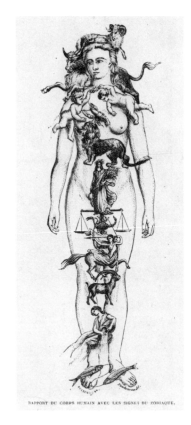

RAPPORT DU CORPS HUMAIN AVEC LES SIGNES DU ZODIAQUE.

This drawing illustrates astrologers' claims that each sign of the zodiac rules, or influences, a part of the human body.

In the second century, Ptolemy argued that the sun and planets revolve around the earth. People accepted this model of the solar system for fourteen centuries.

One of the foremost astronomers and geographers, Claudius Ptolemy, began to make changes in astrology in the second century A.D. He devoted much of his life to the study of astrology and became the world's all-time expert as well as one of astrology's leading influencers. Taking all the different systems of astrology known at the time, Ptolemy reorganized and unified them into a new system. He wrote a number of books explaining his theories, including the *Tetrabiblos*, the first modern astrological textbook. Jennings writes that Ptolemaic astrology is basically the same system followed by astrologers today.

The signs of the zodiac previously had been thought to be ruled by Greek gods. But Ptolemy decided that the planets rule the signs since the planets, unlike gods, are visible to the eye. The sun was widely assumed to be the most important planet. Since it shone at its brightest during Leo, Ptolemy assigned the sun to Leo. Thinking that the moon orbited the closest to the earth and thus was the second most important planet, Ptolemy linked it to the sign next to Leo, Cancer the Crab. With ten signs and five planets remaining, Ptolemy "worked his way around the zodiac wheel in both directions simultaneously," writes Jennings.

Ptolemy's Geocentric View

Despite the many refinements he made to astrology, Ptolemy held to the age-old view of an earth-centered universe. He thought that the earth stood still at the center of the universe while the planets, sun, moon, and stars circled around it. This fit with the Babylonian worldview, that the earth was the focus of the universe and that all the heavenly bodies rotating around it had some significance. Ptolemy's theory did not always fit with the motions of the celestial bodies, but he "thought up clever explanations for what he saw," writes Elizabeth S. Helfman in *Signs & Symbols of the Sun.* Most astronomers continued to accept the view of an earth-centered universe for the next fourteen centuries.

Believing in free will, the Greeks "limited the scope of astrology to certain areas of their lives," writes Lawrence Jerome in *Astrology Disproved.* They confined astrology to indicating favorable times to begin projects and make decisions. But the

Fifteenth-century astronomer Johann de Monte Regio (right) created this model of the world to explain the geocentric theory of Ptolemy (left). It includes the ecliptic of the zodiac, the equator, the north and south poles, and the north and south latitudes known as the Tropic of Cancer and the Tropic of Capricorn.

"[Astrology] enables people to achieve a 'cosmic vision,' move out from our blinkered human viewpoint and . . . grasp the universal processes in a more immediate and comprehensive way."

Dennis Elwell, *Cosmic Loom*

"Astrology . . . speaks to a person's desires and aspirations and gives a cosmic explanation for even the most trivial, inconsequential or idiosyncratic happening in the lives of individuals."

Paul Kurtz, *The Transcendental Temptation*

Romans, who adopted the Greeks' interest in astrology after conquering their nation in the second century B.C., held a very different view. They thought that one's fate could be read in the stars.

Emperors of the Roman Empire paid much attention to the "dictates of the stars" as astrology became intertwined with politics, writes Jerome. "For over 150 years the family of the astrologer Thrasyllus used astrological predictions to manipulate the political decisions . . . during the reigns of nearly every emperor from Tiberius to Domitian," he states. "If Thrasyllus or his son Balbillus said that the stars (or more often comets) indicated blood needed to be spilled, the emperors were all too eager to comply. The astrologers were present in court nearly all the time, and their advice was sought on many if not all issues."

Interest in Astrology Wavers

Not all Romans approved of astrology. Emperor Augustus banned the practice of astrology in A.D. 11. He was afraid that his enemies would use astrology to learn the best time to try to overthrow him. And the Roman senate tried to expel astrologers in a political move to "quell revolutionary ideas," writes Jerome. But for most Romans, astrology played a large part in society. "There are people who cannot appear in public, dine or bathe, without having first consulted the ephemeris," wrote astrologer Juvenal sometime around A.D. 100.

The Romans spread the popularity of astrology throughout the Mediterranean region as their empire blossomed. But around A.D. 180, astrology waned in popularity. "The technical ability to make observations and calculations was lost" at this time, write Derek and Julia Parker in *The Compleat Astrologer*. "As the Roman empire crumbled, astrology descended temporarily into a corrupt superstition," they write.

The barbarians invaded Rome, bringing the so-called Dark Ages, and the study of astrology virtually ceased. The barbarians destroyed books and records of ancient priests who had studied astrology. Eventually, the Roman Catholic church collected and housed existing records of astrology. But, believing it to be a type of magic, the church did not promote it.

While astrology was declining in popularity in Western Europe, it was flourishing in most countries in the Far East. In fact, astrology has tended to remain consistently popular in most Eastern countries, writes Louis MacNeice in *Astrology*. Astrologers were held in great esteem in ancient China. As early as the thirteenth century A.D., Venetian explorer Marco Polo found thousands

An engraving shows ancient Greek philosophers (in medieval European garb) reading the stars while others make calculations in the dust. The rational Greeks, unlike the superstitious Romans, studied astrology without believing that it controlled their fate.

of astrologers in the service of the emperor in the city of Kanbalu, China. They were relied upon to predict everything from epidemics to wars to weather. And in Mongolia, Polo found that wealthy families would not cremate their dead until an astrologer had found a suitable day according to a person's natal chart, even if it meant waiting months, writes MacNeice.

Astrology as Science

As in the Far East, astrology remained popular in Arabia and India. In these countries, astrology was considered a science, writes Branley. Arabians in North Africa and the Eastern Mediterranean can be credited for preserving much of the philosophy and science of astrology. During the European Dark Ages, the Arabians kept alive interest in Ptolemy, including the *Tetrabiblos*, and reintroduced astrology to Europe after the end of the Dark Ages, during the 1100s and 1200s, writes Roy Gallant. Accomplished in the study of astronomy as well as astrology, they set up a major observatory in Baghdad. Arab astrologer Abu Maaschar wrote *Introductorium in Astronomiam* around A.D. 800. This was one of the first books to be translated throughout Europe in the Middle Ages and helped to revive both astrology and astronomy at that time.

In the early Middle Ages, Europeans once again became interested in both astrology and astronomy. Western European royalty turned again to the stargazers for advice about ruling their nations. They valued most the astronomers who also knew about astrology. Consequently, many astronomers cast horoscopes for kings in order to gain the king's financial support for their work in astronomy.

But by the sixteenth century, some Europeans began to poke fun at astrology, writes MacNeice. In 1544, a verse from an English poem called "A Merry Prognostication" had this to say about astrology:

> But I Say if the ninth day of November
> Had fallen upon the tenth day of December
> It had been a marvellous hot year for bees
> For then had the Moon been like a green cheese.

Royalty in medieval and renaissance Europe consulted astrologers and other diviners about their fates. Here, famed sixteenth-century astrologer and fortune-teller Nostradamus casts a magic circle to predict the future of the queen of France, who sees her future within the mirror above the mantelpiece.

Astrology began to wane in popularity during the Reformation, which "cast doubt upon all forms of traditional authority or superstition," writes MacNeice. And as the Renaissance dawned in Western Europe, the "growing spirit of scientific inquiry" also stirred up doubts about astrology as a science.

One scientist in particular played a large role in unsettling long-held beliefs that formed a basis for astrology. In the 1540s, Polish astronomer Nicolaus

Nicolaus Copernicus's sun-centered theory of the solar system replaced Ptolemy's earth-centered theory and thus upset the whole basis of astrology.

Copernicus claimed that the earth did not occupy the center of the universe but circled the sun just like any other planet. He also said that there was no zodiac encircling the earth.

For centuries, astrologers had cherished the belief that the earth sat in the center of the universe. Thinking that all celestial bodies revolved around the earth endowed the stars and planets with significance to ancient people. They imagined that the motion of the planets served some purpose to humanity. Particular movements, such as two planets rising at the same time, seemed to have special meaning.

Explaining Planetary Orbits

Copernicus's theory helped explain the motion of planets. It had puzzled the ancients when the planets seemed to move from west to east and then stop and move backward before resuming their west-to-east motion, writes Branley. Since they had imagined that the planets were gods, they invented reasons for these planetary orbits. Now astronomers explained that the apparent retrograde (backward) motion of planets had nothing to do with gods but resulted because planets revolve at different speeds around the sun. The earth also orbits at different speeds than the other planets. Inner planets Mercury and Venus catch up to earth and pass it. And in time, these planets pass the outer ones. As the lines of sight from one planet to another change, their directions also seem to change, writes Branley.

Branley uses the example of someone riding on a merry-go-round and looking at a distant pole. As the merry-go-round goes to the right, the pole seems to move to the left. As the merry-go-round moves to the left, the pole appears to move to the right. This is how the planets appear to people on earth.

Copernicus's theory was not popular with everyone. The Catholic church "in particular resisted the new idea of a sun-centered system, with

Because Galileo's research proved that the earth revolved around the sun, the Catholic church silenced the Italian scientist and forced him to abandon his study of astronomy.

the earth being just one among numerous minor bodies, because it seemed to imply that earth and man were not God's especial favorites in the universe," writes Jennings.

Italian scientist Galileo Galilei's improvement of the telescope in the 1600s helped astronomers verify their claims. Looking at the sun, Galileo discovered sunspots. These dark spots appeared to move across his lens. This proved that the sun, while not orbiting like the earth and the planets, spun on its own axis. The church actually forbade

The development of the telescope and sextant used by these seventeenth-century astronomers caused the science of astronomy to replace astrology as a focus of study.

Galileo to continue his studies, saying the telescope was the work of the devil. Under the threat of torture, he publicly denounced his findings.

But even the church could not stop the scientific evidence for the new astronomers' findings, which grew like a rolling snowball. Having to accept that the earth was not the center of the universe seemed to threaten belief in astrology. Perhaps the heavenly bodies were not exerting quite as strong an influence as previously imagined since the earth was just another planet. And the invention of the telescope showed that the planets were not as close as the ancients had thought, also making their influence seem less likely. "Astronomy became an important science—man's search to understand the universe," writes Branley. "Astrology remained magic."

Since many could not reconcile astrology with new scientific findings, followers of astrology dwindled during this time, especially in Europe. Until the nineteenth century, the disrepute of astrology continued because of the "scientific revolution," writes MacNeice.

But in the early 1900s, astrology once again came back into public favor. Scientists began to find influences of the heavenly bodies upon nature. For instance, they discovered that rhythms in plants and animals were triggered by the daily and seasonal changes in sunlight, writes Lawrence Jerome. Also, certain aquatic animals were shown to feed and breed in rhythm with the phases of the moon. Studies suggested that sunspots could be connected with everything from economic ups and downs, to the growth of trees, to changes in population in the snowshoe rabbit, he writes. All these celestial influences offered the possibility of astrology having a scientific basis. Interest in it revived.

But despite its renewed popularity, astrology would never again be so interwoven in the fabric of society as it had been in ancient times. Never again would so many civilizations use astrology to predict the welfare of their countries. Never again would the Egyptians use astrology to find the best day and hour for religious ceremonies, nor would the Arabians use it to find the best time to take a journey. Still, more and more people have found a relatively new area of astrology that is meaningful to them. Many are seeking guidance in the stars by having astrologers cast their horoscopes.

"Alone among the sciences, astrology has spanned the centuries and made the journey intact. We shouldn't be surprised that it remains with us, unchanged by time—because astrology is truth—and truth is eternal."

Linda Goodman, *Linda Goodman's Sun Signs*

"Astrology is an ancient form of divination that has changed little since its founding on superstition and ignorance nearly four thousand years ago."

Shawn Carlson, *Experientia*, vol. 44, 1988

Three

Is Astrology Fact or Fantasy?

In 1575, Danish astronomer Tycho Brahe declared that a king would soon be born in Sweden who would conquer lands as far south as Germany. Based on his readings of the stars, he predicted that this king would meet sudden death in the year 1632. At the time, people scoffed at Brahe's prediction. No one believed that a mighty king could come from small, sleepy Sweden.

Twenty-four years after Brahe's prediction, Swedish prince Gustavus Adolphus was born. After Adolphus had become king, the Thirty Years' War erupted in Europe. Championing the cause of Protestantism in this religious war, Adolphus led the Swedish army into battle. Just as Brahe had predicted, Adolphus died in a victorious battle in Germany in 1632.

Is Astrology Accurate?

Throughout history, astrologers have made many ambitious predictions that time has proven true. In ancient times, astrologers prophesied the appearance of the Three Wise Men. In modern times, many pronounced that President John Fitzgerald Kennedy would not live out his term in office.

Most people have heard the phrase "Beware the

(opposite page) An astrologer works in his study. Would his predictions actually come true?

Sixteenth-century Danish astronomer Tycho Brahe (left) accurately predicted the birth and death of Swedish ruler Gustavus Adolphus (right).

Ides of March." This is what astrologer Spurinna said to Julius Caesar, then the emperor of Rome, in the year 44 B.C. Because of what he read in the stars, Spurinna warned Caesar to be careful on March 15, which the Romans called the Ides of March. Caesar stayed in his house most of the day until his colleague Brutus convinced him to visit the Senate chambers. A few hours later, Caesar was stabbed to death by a group of senators.

False Predictions

While astrologers claim to have made many accurate predictions throughout the ages, skeptics say they can find just as many—or more—examples of predictions that have not come true.

For instance, many astrologers have decreed that the world would end. So far, each such prediction has been wrong.

On occasion, astrologers' wrong predictions have caused great panic. For example, in the 1500s, several astrologers proclaimed that Europe would be dangerously flooded. German astrologer Johann Stoeffler was one who said that the floods would be so severe as to destroy the world. People built arks and boats in preparation for the crisis. Some abandoned their homes in search of higher land.

What actually occurred in 1524? Not a disastrous flood—not even a major one. There was only heavier than usual rainfall in much of Europe that year.

In modern times, Indian astrologers also caused needless panic. They proclaimed that a catastrophe of some kind would occur between February 3 and 5 in 1962. Gary Jennings, author of *The Teenager's Realistic Guide to Astrology*, quotes one astrologer as saying, "The next three days will see the earth bathed in the blood of thousands of kings."

The Indian population bought insurance policies and lucky charm bracelets to prepare for the disaster. Thousands of Indians fled their homes to hide in the hills or pray in temples. But the days of February 3 through 5 came and went without

A group of Roman senators assassinates Julius Caesar on the Ides of March in 44 B.C. Caesar's astrologer had warned him of ill fortune on that day.

"We are part of this whole solar system, and somehow we are uniquely imprinted at birth. We are somehow synchronized to the celestial patterns that were present at our birth. It's not that the planets are doing it *to* us, it's that we're synchronized *with* them."

Astrologer Linda Hill, New York

"From the astronomer's point of view, astrology is meaningless, unnecessary, and impossible to explain if we accept the broad set of physical laws we have conceived over the years to explain what happens on the Earth and in the sky. Astrology snipes at the roots of all pure science. Moreover, astrology patently doesn't work."

Astronomer Jay Pasachoff, *Contemporary Astronomy*

incident. Some said that no disaster had occurred because astrologers had warned the people in time. Therefore, Indians had been able to "conduct thousands of public prayer sessions before the day of doom and their prayers invoked the power of the gods to ward off evil," writes Jennings.

Do astrologers make more false than true predictions? Astronomers Roger Culver and Philip Ianna, authors of *The Gemini Syndrome*, tracked more than three thousand predictions made by well-known astrologers over a five-year period. The authors found that only about eleven percent of the predictions astrologers made during that time came true. Many of the predictions counted in this eleven percent were barely correct. This included predictions with vague wording, such as "There will be a tragedy in the northern United States during winter." Another prediction said that SALT talks (talks between the United States and the Soviet Union about defense weapons) might be stalled for another year. This type of prediction may have resulted more from the astrologer's shrewd guessing than from guidance from the stars, say the authors. Examples of false predictions give skeptics ammunition to claim that astrology is nonsense. Astrology is based on superstition, not on scientific evidence, they say.

Science Versus Symbolism

Much of what is believed about astrology today can be traced to the symbolic and supernatural interpretations the ancients made of their universe. From the naming of the signs of the zodiac to ascribing characteristics to the planets, the ancients drew richly on their imaginations. For example, many of the zodiac constellations do not even look like the symbols the ancients decided that they represented. H. J. Eysenck and D. K. B. Nias, authors of *Astrology: Science or Superstition?*, performed an experiment showing that most people cannot identify the various signs of the zodiac as the scorpion, ram, and other symbols they are supposed to look like. When people were shown pictures of various constellations and asked to name the corresponding sign of the zodiac, no one scored better than chance, say the authors.

James Kaler, astronomy professor at the University of Illinois, criticizes astrologers for their way of attributing certain qualities to the various planets. "The ancients believed that the planets were gods. And the so-called character of the planets comes entirely from the gods they were named after," he says. Because Mars was the god of war, this planet is associated with a warlike nature. Since the goddess Venus represents love and beauty, astrologers linked this planet to a love of the arts.

"In reality, the personalities of these planets are entirely switched," says Kaler. Mars, with its low

The red color of the planet Mars may have inspired ancient astrologers to name it after the god of war and to attribute an aggressive personality to those born under its influence.

atmospheric pressure, is a friendly planet compared to Venus. Venus is an "absolute hell," he says, with a crushing atmospheric pressure one hundred times that of earth. It has sulfuric acid rainfalls and a surface temperature of 800 degrees Fahrenheit.

Ptolemy also made assumptions about the planets that were not based on fact, write Eysenck and Nias. Because he thought Mars was near the sun, Ptolemy decided that this hot, arid planet had a drying influence. Since the moon was closest to the earth, it supposedly absorbed moisture and had an effect opposite that of Mars. In fact, Mars has much more moisture than the moon, which is quite dry.

Ptolemy also used faulty reasoning when he assigned planets to rule signs of the zodiac, say his critics. All of the planets move through the constellations at various times of the year. But Ptolemy decreed that each constellation needed its own ruling planet. His assignment of ruling planets seems far too arbitrary to have any real signifi-

This world map drawn by fifth-century B.C. Greek historian Herodotus shows a lack of knowledge of any land south of the equator. The principles of astrology were developed within such a worldview and thus, critics say, exclude anyone born in the Southern Hemisphere.

cance, say his critics.

"Even assuming that the planets and the constellations do exert varying influences on the earth and its earthlings, we might think it a little unlikely that the influences of the ruling planets and the signs they rule should be so neatly matched—considering the way Ptolemy shuffled the planets around the zodiac wheel, like dealing hands in a card game," writes Jennings.

Astrology and the Southern Hemisphere

Scientists also criticize Ptolemy for distorting astrology for people in the Southern Hemisphere. When he was deciding which planets rule which constellations, he did not know that one-half of the earth existed south of the equator. Ptolemy decided that the sun should rule Leo since it is brightest when it is in that constellation. But the seasons are reversed in the Southern Hemisphere, and there the sun is not nearly at its height when in Leo.

What is more, anyone born in the "No-Man's Land" around the earth's North Pole cannot have a horoscope, says Kaler. "When you go above the Arctic Circle, the ecliptic and part of the zodiac disappears below the horizon," he says. "That means you can't have a zodiac sign if you live in this area." Take an example of someone born on December 25 in Barrow, Alaska, which is north of the Arctic Circle. At this location, the sun is so far from the equator that it would never rise above the horizon, says Harry Shipman, astronomy professor at the University of Delaware. The ascendant sign also could not rise above the horizon in this location. So the standard methods of charting a horoscope for this person born in Alaska could not be used.

Much of what is believed about astrology today is based on other inaccurate knowledge the ancients had about their universe. They thought the earth was flat and that all planets revolved around it. For centuries, they imagined that stars were clumped

"I have never heard of a single person who attacked astrology on real scientific grounds."

John Manolesco, *Scientific Astrology*

"[Astrologists] will not acknowledge honestly the decisive fact that their futile practices have been investigated with the greatest care and impartiality by the foremost scholars of the leading Western nations for almost three centuries, and not one of these has failed to condemn them."

Robert Eisler, *The Royal Art of Astrology*

A drawing of the constellations most familiar to the ancients. Before the invention of the telescope, people believed the stars in constellations were actually clumped together as they appear in the sky. They did not know that the stars are actually light-years apart.

closely in neat patterns known as constellations. In fact, stars are far flung and only *appear* to be grouped together. In the constellation of Leo, for example, the star called Denebola, positioned at the lion's tail, is two hundred billion miles from earth, says Shipman. Leo's brightest star, Regulus, situated at the opposite end of the lion from Denebola, near the front of the lion's body, is a phenomenal four hundred billion miles from earth.

A Changing View of the Universe

The ancients also seriously miscalculated the distances of planets from earth. When they gazed into the sky, they thought the planets moved within the signs of the zodiac and were only a few miles overhead. But today we know that the stars and planets lie millions of miles from earth. Moving within the solar system, the planets are not even close to the constellations they supposedly rule.

In modern times, now that spacecraft have traveled to the planets and have explored them in some detail, our view of the universe should be very different from that of ancient astrologers, says Andrew Fraknoi, executive officer of the Astronomical Society of the Pacific. "We now know that the stars are not mystic lights or the playthings of the gods, but nothing more and nothing less than other suns, unimaginably large and hot, incredibly remote, and mercifully unconcerned with the daily lives of the creatures who inhabit planet Earth," he says. There is simply no evidence that celestial objects influence humans in such a specific and personal way as astrologers claim, adds Fraknoi.

Scientists question the claim made by many astrologers that the gravitational force of the planets affects a baby at birth. They say that any so-called planetary influences would be extraordinarily weak

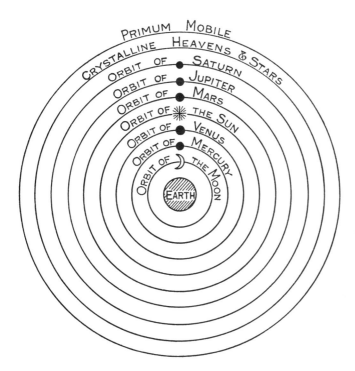

The orbits of the planets, moon, and sun as seen in a geocentric view of the universe.

by the time they reach earth. The fluorescent lights overhead in the hospital room are more powerful than the radiation of the planets, Kaler says. Scientists have calculated that the obstetrician who delivers a baby has about six times the gravitational pull of Mars and about two thousand billion times its tidal force, says Fraknoi.

When Does Life Begin?

Scientists also wonder why astrologers consider a person's moment of birth, rather than conception, a crucial time. "When astrology was set up long ago, the moment of birth was considered the magic creation point of life," says Fraknoi. "But today, we understand birth as the culmination of nine months of steady development inside the womb. Indeed, scientists now believe that many aspects of a child's personality are set long before birth."

Scientists doubt the accuracy of using the time of birth for astrology, since many cannot agree on what is actually the exact moment. Is it when the baby takes its first breath? When the head of the baby passes out of the mother's womb? Scientists question how the moment of birth should be determined for an induced delivery or for a baby delivered by cesarean section. These deliveries probably do not coincide with what would have been the baby's natural birth time. Does this mean that a parent could, to some extent, shape a child's horoscope by selecting a favorable time and inducing birth?

An area which probably causes the most criticism of astrology by scientists has to do with a phenomenon called "precession of the equinoxes." Precession refers to the movement of the earth over time, in addition to its rotation and revolution. Like a spinning top, the earth's axis swings around in space in a circle. It completes a circle about once every twenty-six thousand years. The sun, moon, and planets continue to orbit within the same band of sky. But the earth points to different parts of the sky over the centuries because of its wobbling orbit. The effect of this is that the seasons of the year very gradually change their beginning and ending dates.

Skeptics of astrology say that many astrologers do not take into account that precession has thrown off the signs of the zodiac by roughly three weeks. For instance, the traditional astrological calendar says that someone born between March 21 and April 20 has Aries for his or her sun sign. But because of the precession of the equinox, the sun now enters Pisces on about March 14 and does not move into Aries until about April 12.

Even so, most astrologers today continue to follow the traditional zodiac dates, called the tropical zodiac. The tropical zodiac follows the dates of the vernal equinox observed by the ancients. It defines the zodiac in terms of the time of year and ignores the actual positions of the sun and constellations relative to each other.

A Tendency to Cling to Tradition

That most astrologers continue to follow the tropical zodiac shows their tendency to cling to tradition and ignore the facts, say critics. "Zodiacal signs have no existence apart from the constellations that inspired their invention," writes Gary Jennings. "A zodiacal sign is an imaginary picture that the ancients saw in a certain group of stars." Scientist Ivan Kelly, of the Committee for the Scientific Investigation of Claims of the Paranormal, also criticizes this method. "The zodiac signs are now no longer related to the actual constellations after which they were named thousands of year ago, he says. "Instead, the space which has been assigned to the zodiac signs must somehow possess a set of influences of its own."

A minority of astrologers compensate for the precession of the equinoxes. They use the sidereal zodiac, which adjusts the signs for the three-week

"Astrology has not been proved by laboratory tests . . . but the answer to scientific skepticism is that astrology has never been disproved. It is a subject belonging to the realm of demonstrable fact. That, in my estimation, demonstrates its reliability."

Myra Kingsley, astrologer

"The modern concepts of astronomy and astrophysics give no support—better said, negative support—to the tenets of astrology."

Bart Bok, *The Humanist,* September 1975

shift of the constellations. For example, the tropical zodiac considers March 21 to April 20 to be ruled by the sign Aries, while the sidereal zodiac says Aries is preeminent April 13 to May 13.

The "New" Planets

Another criticism scientists frequently make about astrology is its handling of the discovery of the planets Uranus, Neptune, and Pluto. They were not discovered until 1781, 1846, and 1930, respectively, at which times astrologers added them to their science.

As the first new planet to be discovered after thousands of years, Uranus created a lot of excitement and confusion among astrologers. Since Ptolemy had already assigned all previously known planets to signs of the zodiac, many astrologers puzzled over how to include Uranus. Some astrologers wanted to have Uranus co-rule Aquarius with the planet Saturn, while others wanted to ignore it altogether. Today, astrologers still do not have uniform agreement about this.

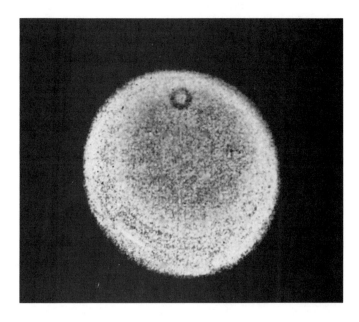

Uranus was discovered by astronomer William Herschel in 1781 and bore his name at first. Only after being dubbed Uranus for the Greek god of the sky did astrologers determine its astrological qualities.

The planet Neptune, discovered in 1846, was given astrological rulership over Pisces the Fish because Neptune was god of the sea.

When the planet Uranus was discovered, it was initially named after the scientist who discovered it, William Herschel. All of the existing planets in astrology have taken on qualities of gods they were named after. But astrologers could not think of what qualities to associate with this new planet until it was renamed after the Greek god of the sky, Uranus. Astrologers interpreted the presence of Uranus in a person's horoscope as representing upheaval and disruption because the planet's discovery came unexpectedly, writes Jennings.

Sixty-five years later, astronomers discovered the planet Neptune. Because Neptune was the god of the sea, many astrologers decided it could co-rule Pisces with the planet Jupiter. Astrologers associated watery qualities like vagueness, dreaminess, and instability with Neptune, writes Jennings.

The planet Pluto, identified in 1930, was so far away from the sun that astronomers named it after

Pluto (foreground), identified in 1930, was named after the Greek god of the underworld because it is the farthest of the planets from the sun. The realm of the god Pluto probably inspired astrologers to assign the planet rulership of Scorpio, the sign related to death.

the Roman god of the underworld, Pluto. Qualities represented by Pluto became violence, cataclysm, and overthrow. This planet was so identified because its discovery occurred during the Second World War, writes Jennings. Astrologers who decided that Pluto should rule a sign of the zodiac matched it to Scorpio, another turbulent sign.

"Serious astrologers claim that the influence of all the major bodies in the solar system must be taken into account to arrive at an accurate horoscope," says Andrew Fraknoi. "But weren't all horoscopes cast before 1930 incorrect, since astrologers were not including an important planet? Moreover, why did the problems or inaccuracies in early horoscopes not lead astrologers to 'sense' the presence of these planets long before astronomers discovered them?"

The different ways astrologers regard the newer planets is just one example of their inconsistency, say astronomers. Others question why astrologers study the planets and stars in great depth but ignore the influence of very distant stars, galaxies, and quasars. "Billions of stupendous bodies all over the universe should add their influence to that of our tiny little sun, moon, and planets," says Fraknoi.

The fact that astrologers seem unable to agree about a lot of facts does not help their image in scientists' eyes. After thousands of years of perfecting their art, different schools of astrology disagree on how to cast and interpret a horoscope, says Fraknoi. "You can have your horoscope cast and read by different astrologers on the very same day and get completely different predictions, interpretations, or suggestions," he says. "If astrology were a science—as astrologers claim— you would expect that the same experiment or calculation would always give the same result."

The Heavenly Bodies and Nature

Astrologers respond to their critics by pointing to scientific studies documenting the influence of celestial bodies on earth and its inhabitants. Scientists have found that many vital functions of plants and animals—including breathing and reproduction—are influenced by the sun and the moon in species ranging from potatoes to flatworms. Scientists refer to the aspects of behavior that are influenced by heavenly bodies as biological clocks or circadian (one-day) rhythms.

The solar system is a place of many rhythms, including the rhythm of day and night, the recurrence of seasons, and the fluctuation of tides, writes Roy A. Gallant in *Astrology: Sense or Nonsense?* Many animals gear their activities in accordance with these rhythms. For example, bats, moths, and hamsters are nocturnal, or active at night, whereas people, dogs, and butterflies are active during the day. Green plants respond to the rhythms of the solar system by leaning toward

"Astrology may succeed where both science and religion have failed: to give each human being a true picture of his own uniqueness in what seems to be a vast, chaotic, and often hostile universe."

Michael Zeilik, *American Journal of Physics*, July 1974

"The world is advancing with the assistance of science and technology. . . . If we are to cope with the complicated problems of our time, then we need to use the best critical intelligence we can muster, and not seek to escape into a superstitious mythology that originated in our primitive past, when we still huddled around the campfire, afraid of the night."

Andrew Fraknoi, astronomer and executive officer of the Astronomical Society of the Pacific

This bat sleeps during the day and is active at night. Astrologers contend that the rhythms of the sun, moon, and other celestial phenomena influence human, animal, and plant behavior. Science is discovering that this may indeed be true.

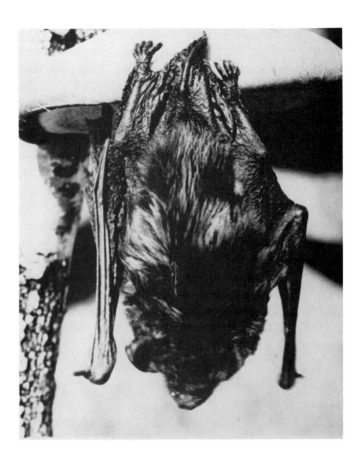

sunlight, which enables them to produce sugar, writes Gallant.

As an example of an animal responding to its biological clock, Gallant describes how the *Palolo viridis* worm synchronizes its breeding with the lunar cycle. This worm has an annual "swarming date," when it appears in large numbers to mate, seven to nine days after a full moon in November or December. The posterior parts of the worms break off and float to the surface of the sea where they wriggle around in swarms. The body walls rupture, with male worms releasing sperm and female worms releasing eggs. After fertilization, new individual worms are formed.

Scientists can cite other examples of lunar influences on nature. Oysters open and shut their shells in a distinct rhythm. For many years, scientists believed oysters acted in rhythm with the ocean tides, feeding at high tide when covered by water and protectively closing their shells at low tide when exposed to air. An experiment was performed to find out if this was true. Oysters were removed from the sea and taken to a lab far inland. To the scientists' surprise, the oysters changed their rhythm. They began to open and shut in time with various phases of the moon. "Patterns of behavior in oysters . . . which were once attributed to the pull of the tides are now known to result from the changing position of the Moon, new or full," write astrologers Derek and Julia Parker, authors of *The New Compleat Astrologer.*

Biologist Frank A. Brown, Jr., of Northwestern University in Evanston, Illinois, says of the oyster experiment: "The only plausible explanation is that these creatures are obtaining information as to the Moon's position through some subtle channels." He adds that "some common subtle rhythmic information" from the lunar cycle affects the "activity or metabolism of organisms as different as potatoes, seaweed, carrots, earthworms, salamanders, and mice."

The Moon's Influence on People

What about lunar influences on humans? American scientist E. M. Dewan theorized that the moon once regulated the timing of women's menstrual cycles by acting as a planetary clock, and that many women have become irregular in their periods because artificial and irregular light has replaced the moon's light. To test his theory, Dewan had twenty women with chronically irregular menstrual cycles leave a bedroom light on for three nights after the fourteenth day of their menstrual cycle. The "moon substitute" proved successful, with all of these women regulating their menstruation.

For some time, people have alleged a connection between phases of the moon and certain activities of people. "The word 'lunacy' has as its root the Latin *luna* (for moon) and comes from observations that mental patients were particularly restless during full moon," writes Gallant. Members of some police departments believe that many criminal acts of violence increase with the occurrence of the full moon, writes an astrologist called Zolar in *The History of Astrology.*

But many scientists say that there is no statistical proof of such a lunar influence on human beings. Professor Harry Shipman, an astronomer at the University of Delaware, has looked at the correlation between lunar phases and crime statistics. He found no link between full moons and incidents of violence.

Professor James Kaler believes that a tendency to overestimate coincidences may explain why

Does a full moon drive some people mad? Scientists have gathered evidence to support the belief that the cycles of the moon regulate many biological functions, from the activity of earthworms to the menstrual cycles of women.

some people link violent behavior with phases of the moon. Because many people have heard about strange behavior during a full moon, they will be more likely to notice any such behavior that occurs. But people may also not notice events that contradict their beliefs, such as times when nothing out of the ordinary happens during a full moon.

Magnetic Forces

Through what mechanisms do astrologers believe heavenly bodies affect life on earth? How can they link events like the movement of two planets and the birth of a human being?

Some scientists and astrologers believe celestial bodies send off magnetic signals that affect both humans and animals. The entire earth is essentially a magnet with magnetic poles at the North and South poles. These poles attract charged particles that enter the earth's atmosphere. An area called the magnetic force field shields the earth from radiation by deflecting weaker, charged particles. The magnetic field of the earth is roughly twenty to thirty times larger than the earth itself, writes Gallant.

Planets send off electromagnetic waves, called radiation. Radiation varies from low frequency, long wavelengths, to high frequency, short wavelengths. The latter type of waves, short and highly penetrating, can be either a gamma ray or an X ray. Scientists have found many sources of X rays and some sources of gamma rays in the universe. For example, X rays were recently discovered in the Crab nebula. Astronomers now know that all stars emit ultraviolet radiation. And the sun and Jupiter are sources of microwave radiation.

Many of these electromagnetic waves that strike the earth are repelled, but some high-energy waves are able to penetrate its atmosphere. Once in the atmosphere, these emissions can cause a change in the strength of the earth's magnetic field. This

"Astrology is the science of observing the movements of the Planets and discerning the relationships between those movements and the course of human lives. . . . It is the most ancient, most validated, most followed tool of self-awareness yet devised by humanity."

Astrologer Grant Lewi, *Astrology for the Millions*

"As a field of knowledge, astrology is a quagmire of contradictions."

Shawn Carlson, *Experientia*, vol. 44, 1988

occurrence is called a geomagnetic electrical storm, which may be evidenced by telephone and television interference and by curtains of light near the earth's magnetic poles called auroras. The solar wind can create enough changes in the pressure of earth's magnetic field to affect both humans and animals. Sunspots, or dark patches that appear on the sun's surface about every eleven years, are actually gaseous material erupting from inside the sun. Sunspots whip up the sun's solar wind, resulting in even greater electromagnetic activity on earth, writes Gallant.

Mental Patients and Celestial Activity

Some scientists have found a connection between the occurrence of sunspots and more excitable, aggressive behavior in mental patients. Investigators at Douglas Hospital in Montreal kept records of the times when the more excitable and violent behavior of these patients occurred. Because the bizarre behavior could not be explained in terms of foods, medications, or other factors, investigators looked for a connection to nature. Weather factors such as humidity, temperature, and barometric pressure were also eliminated.

Finally, Dr. Heinz Lehmann from the hospital consulted astronomers at the U.S. Space Disturbance Forecast Center in Boulder, Colorado, for a record of the sun's activity during the times of the patients' outbursts. Medical scientists who studied this situation found an apparent connection between the outbursts of patients, sunspot activity, and geomagnetic disturbance. Sunspots can cause changes in the earth's magnetic field, so such a correlation is not impossible, say the scientists who studied this incident. Since sun storms can cause a compass needle to deviate, then possibly the equally sensitive human brain could also respond to magnetic disturbance.

Some humans are able to find north without the

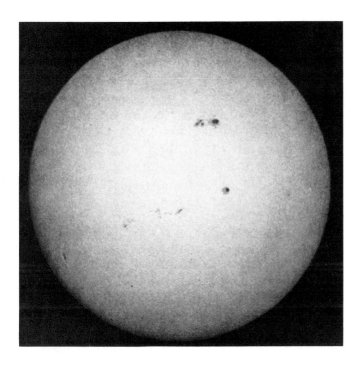

Sunspots are dark patches that appear on the sun's surface in regular eleven-year cycles. Their effect on earth's magnetic field is sometimes quite dramatic.

use of a compass or any other obvious clues, notes astronomer Seymour Percy. Animals also perceive and react to magnetic cues: Ocean-dwelling bacteria use magnetism to guide them downward to the food supply, and birds navigate by the magnetic field.

Percy also believes that magnetism may be the "signal that calls the fetus from the womb." His theory is as follows: On magnetically disturbed days, the fetus may receive its signals through the cells of its nervous system, which serve as antennae. The baby may have magnetic antennae sensitive to the same frequencies and resonances as its parents. The baby possibly waits for a magnetic signal from the planets before it is born.

Seymour theorizes that the "positions of the planets set off magnetic signals that children are waiting to hear as their cues to enter the world." Therefore, it is no accident that the child is born with certain planets in certain positions.

Critics of astrology, knowing of vast distances between celestial bodies and earth, believe it unlikely that heavenly bodies could exert a gravitational, magnetic, or other force strong enough to influence human behavior. "All the long-range forces we know in the universe get weaker as objects get farther apart," says Andrew Fraknoi, executive officer of the Astronomical Society of the Pacific. "But as you might expect in an earth-centered system made thousands of years ago, astrological influences do not depend on distance at all. The importance of Mars in your horoscope is identical whether the planet is on the same side of the Sun as the Earth or seven times farther away on the other side."

Magnetic Fields of Different Strengths

Professor Harry Shipman, an astronomer at the University of Delaware, wonders why astrologers do not weigh the strength of the planets' magnetic fields in determining the relative astrological importance of each. The strength of each planet's magnetic field varies considerably: Mars has a weak magnetic field, and Jupiter and Saturn have the strongest magnetic fields, he says. Thus, he suggests, Jupiter and Saturn should have a stronger influence on all of us than Mars should.

Nonetheless, Shipman seems more open than other scientists to the possibility of unseen influences of the planets on life on earth. "I'm uncomfortable hearing astronomers say that they don't know of any forces that could make astrology work," says Shipman. "There could always be fundamental forces that we haven't discovered yet."

Before revelations of various types of radiation, "it was only too easy to dismiss astrology as being false simply because there were no obvious emissions or vibrations which could account for it," write Derek and Julia Parker.

But even with some evidence of planetary influence, Shipman cannot reach the conclusion that

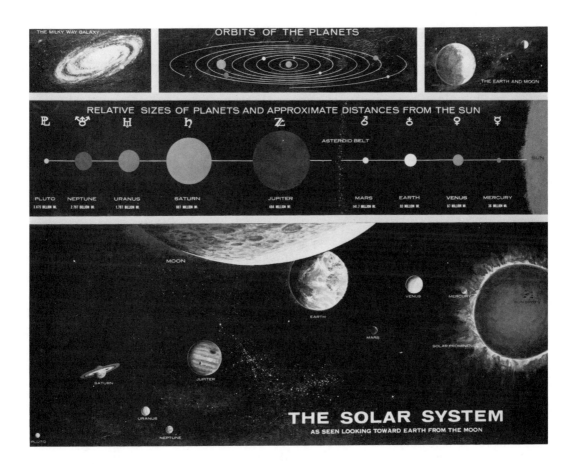

THE MILKY WAY GALAXY

ORBITS OF THE PLANETS

THE EARTH AND MOON

RELATIVE SIZES OF PLANETS AND APPROXIMATE DISTANCES FROM THE SUN

ASTEROID BELT

SUN

PLUTO	NEPTUNE	URANUS	SATURN	JUPITER	MARS	EARTH	VENUS	MERCURY
3,675 BILLION MI.	2,797 BILLION MI.	1,787 BILLION MI.	887 MILLION MI.	484 MILLION MI.	141.7 MILLION MI.	93 MILLION MI.	67 MILLION MI.	36 MILLION MI.

MOON

VENUS

MERCURY

SUN SPOTS

EARTH

MARS

SOLAR PROMINENCE

SATURN

JUPITER

THE SOLAR SYSTEM

AS SEEN LOOKING TOWARD EARTH FROM THE MOON

URANUS

NEPTUNE

PLUTO

astrology works. As a scientist, he knows that cosmic rays from the sun have some effect. "That's not to say that having the planet Mars over the eastern horizon when you were born means you will be a good soldier," says Shipman.

Like all scientists, it puzzles Shipman that oysters seem to know when to open and shut their shells, or that certain types of bacteria know to swim northward. "We don't understand the biochemical mechanisms that allow animals and organisms to do these things," he says. "But that doesn't mean we have to appeal to some kind of astro-rays from the moon to explain these phenomena." Shipman does not think the moon's

The gravitational and electromagnetic fields of the sun, planets, and moon influence the earth. But given the great distances between planets, can these influences affect people as strongly as astrologers claim?

"Astrology is a system of scientific calculation. The interpretations that derive from this are based on traditional empirical references that have established their validity through centuries of time."

Gary Keen, *Spiritual, Metaphysical, and New Trends in Modern Astrology*

"Every attempt, whether of astrologers or scientists, to produce the evidence of the validity of astrological laws has been in vain. It is now quite certain that the signs in the sky which presided over our births have no power whatever to decide our fates, to affect our hereditary characteristics, or play any part however humble in the totality of affects, random and otherwise, which form the fabric of our lives and mold our impulses to action. Confronted with science, modern and traditional astrology are seen to be imaginary doctrines."

Michel Gauquelin, *Scientific Basis of Astrology*

influence explains why oysters open and shut their shells the way they do. Oysters probably synchronize their movements by waiting a certain number of hours to open or shut their shells, according to an internal clock, he says.

Still, even today scientists do not know about all of the various electromagnetic waves radiated by heavenly bodies. Many of these radioactive waves were not discovered until recently because they are absorbed in the upper reaches of the universe and are not visible to the human eye. Scientists need sophisticated telescopes to detect such radiation.

In time, scientists may unravel the mysteries of exactly which radiations come from which celestial bodies and how this radiation might affect humans and other organisms. Someday, scientists may also understand the forces that signal organisms to mate at certain times or migrate in certain directions. But until that time, astrologers and scientists will continue to circle around this debate like planets in orbit.

Experiments in Astrology

Many scientists say that astrologers have failed to produce evidence to prove that astrology works. In hundreds of experiments, scientists have tried to find links between personality traits and sun signs and planets. The results are decidedly mixed.

Most of the best known experiments were conducted by French psychologist Michel Gauquelin. The fact that he is both a scientist and a statistician makes his studies especially worth noting. In one experiment, Gauquelin decided to test the theory of prominent sixteenth-century astronomer and scientist Johannes Kepler. Kepler was looking for similarities in the positions of the planets at the time of birth among parents and children. Kepler's findings: Children and one or both parents are likely to be born with the same planet at their ascendant or at their midheaven. If both parents were born with a

Prominent sixteenth-century German astronomer Johannes Kepler looked for similarities in the horoscopes of parents and their children. He found that the parents and their children often had the same planet influencing their personalities.

certain planet in a certain position, then their children are twice as likely to be born with this same planet present. Gauquelin studied fifteen thousand couples and their children. He reached the same conclusions as Kepler.

Gauquelin's experiment showed that planetary positions are more important that one's sun sign. For instance, when looking for correlations between choice of career and sun sign, he would have expected to find a higher-than-average number of politicians born under the sign Aries. This sign supposedly indicates leadership skills. But upon studying the birth records of politicians, Gauquelin did not find a high number of politicians born under Aries.

However, Gauquelin was able to find correlations between choice of careers and the position of some *planets*. He found a high number of politicians born when the planet Jupiter was either rising or reaching its zenith at the moment of birth. He found a high presence of Saturn in the charts of doctors and scientists. Saturn is associated with a reflective temperament. He studied the charts of military leaders, athletes, and top executives, finding an above-average presence of Mars rising or passing its zenith at their moment of birth. Named after the god of war, Mars represents a brave, belligerent, and dynamic personality.

Other Studies

Gauquelin repeated his experiments over and over on different groups of people, often finding support for a correspondence between planetary personalities and careers chosen by people born under certain planets. But other scientists who performed similar experiments came up with different results.

For instance, professors James T. Bennett and James R. Barth of George Washington University examined the horoscopes of men who re-enlisted in the Marines. They looked for a prominence of Mars in these men. They found no trends favoring astrological signs ruled by Mars.

Physicist John McGervey from Case Western Reserve University researched the birthdays of 6,475 politicians and 16,634 prominent scientists. He expected that they would cluster among certain signs of the zodiac. But the physicist did not find any relationship between the politicians and scientists and their zodiac signs.

Some scientists say they have proven that horoscopes are not reliable in predicting personality characteristics. Physicist Shawn Carlson of the Lawrence Berkeley Laboratory asked several leading astrologers in Europe and the United States to match the profiles of 116 people with their horoscopes. The astrologers were given one horoscope and three personality profiles, one of which belonged to the subject of the horoscope.

The astrologers predicted that they would match the profile with the correct person more than fifty percent of the time. However, the astrologers could only find the correct profile thirty-four percent of the time, as often as guessing. Five similar tests have been run since 1980 with the same negative results, says Fraknoi.

Gauquelin also had doubts about the accuracy

A depiction of Mars, god of war, from an astrology book. Characteristics of and things related to Mars are listed beneath the drawing. Modern researchers found that the natal horoscopes of Marines who re-enlisted did not show a prominent Martian influence as expected.

of horoscopes. In one experiment, he sent the horoscope for one of the worst mass murderers in French history to 150 people. He told them it was their own horoscope and asked how well it described them. Ninety-four percent of the subjects said they recognized themselves in the horoscope!

Why do people tend to believe horoscopes that are identified as their own? Apparently horoscopes work because they are filled with general statements that will apply to many individuals. Fraknoi describes an experiment performed by psychologist C. R. Snyder and his associates at the University of Kansas. It shows that people tend to believe general descriptions when they are told the descriptions apply to them, especially when they are told that the descriptions are their horoscopes.

The psychologists created a fake personality description containing phrases people most often use to describe themselves. They showed it to three

Studies have shown that people will see themselves accurately described in almost any horoscope if they believe it is theirs.

groups of people who were asked to rate how well the description applied to them, on a scale of one to five. One represented the least accurate and five the most accurate.

All three groups were given different information about the personality description. The first group was told that the profile was a general sketch that was true for all people. The second group was asked for their month of birth and were told that the profile was a horoscope. The third group was asked for the day on which they were born and were told that the profile was their personal horoscope. The results: The first group rated the description 3.2 for accuracy; the second group rated the description 3.76; and the third group, 4.38.

Vague Statements and Generalities

Other experiments have come up with similar results. One Australian researcher reversed the readings of twenty-two people, giving them the opposite of what they were supposed to be. Asked if the reading applied to them, all of the people said it did. Thus, people tend to identify themselves with general descriptions, however unfounded, that they believe apply to them. David Marks and Richard Kammann explain in their book *The Psychology of the Psychic*:

> Our personalities are not as fixed and constant as we usually imagine. Everybody is shy in one situation, bold in another, clever at one task, bumbling at another, generous one day, selfish the next. Thus, we can usually find aspects of ourselves that will match up with a vague statement, although the specific examples of self will be different from one person to the next.

If a person's horoscope says, "You have a great need for other people to like and admire you," he or she can probably recall a time of wanting to be more popular, say Marks and Kammann. But if this horoscope said nearly the opposite, like "you don't

"Astrology is scientific in this sense: It's based on astronomy, the same way a doctor bases his predictions on computer-gathered statistics. Only I think astrology is more reliable than those two."

Astrologer Joan Quigley

"[Astrology] sounds a lot like science. It's got technical terms. . . . It's got jargon. . . . [But] the fact is, there's no theory for it, there are no observational data for it. . . . Nobody's ever found any validity to it at all."

Astronomer Richard Berendzen, American University

need other people to be your true self," the same person could probably recall an experience when he or she enjoyed being alone. Life has so many diverse moments that most people can recall events that agree with a horoscope, no matter what it says, conclude the authors.

One group of scientists describes this tendency to believe vague, ambiguous, and general statements as descriptive of one's personality as the "Barnum effect." This name comes from the late circus owner, P. T. Barnum, who once said, "There's a sucker born every minute." Barnum also "maintained that his secret of success was always to have a little something for everyone," according to an article called "Belief in Astrology," from the *Skeptical Inquirer*, Winter 1991. The authors of the article say that horoscope profiles contain an assortment of statements in which everyone can see something of themselves.

According to this article, most horoscopes mix

An astrologer's tools include books listing planetary positions, guides for interpreting charts, horoscope blanks, a globe, and a protractor for determining and drawing angles between planets. But the skill and experience to interpret the data accurately is perhaps an astrologer's most important tool.

general statements with specific ones. People are so impressed by the specific statements that fit that they tend to pay less attention to ones that do not. The general statements, say the authors, "provide readily acceptable 'padding.'" Many horoscopes also contain "double-headed" statements like "You are generally cheerful and optimistic but get depressed at times," again statements that describe nearly everyone, says the *Skeptical Inquirer* article.

Is astrology fact or fantasy? Astrologers and scientists will probably never cease debating this question.

Four

Does Astrology Work?

Throughout the centuries, controversy has enveloped astrology as thickly as the gases swirling around the planet Venus.

Saying that astrologers were quacks trying to cheat gullible people, the Romans tried to drive out astrologers in 139 B.C. Offended by the notion that the stars and planets—rather than God—were the governors of one's future, the Christian church outlawed the practice of astrology around A.D. 400. Adolf Hitler consulted astrologers about military strategy during World War II but had them deported to concentration camps when they predicted his defeat. In 1976 in the United States, 186 scientists were alarmed enough about the claims of astrologers to strongly denounce the authenticity of astrology in a report in *The Humanist* magazine.

Is Astrology a Menace?

Many scientists insist that astrology is a menace that harms individuals who rely on it. "Believers in astrology try to ignore reality," says James Kaler, astronomy professor at the University of Illinois. "They say that their fate is in the stars. That makes them feel that they don't have to take responsibility for their actions. And that's why astrology is wrong."

(opposite page) A Buddhist monk mixes high technology with religion to determine what the heavens portend for the day.

Former president Ronald Reagan is said to have arranged his daily schedule to harmonize with the predictions of an astrologer. Was he acting wisely or foolishly?

There *are* those people who take horoscopes so seriously that they may hesitate to leave their house if the stars portend a difficult day. Former president Ronald Reagan refused to talk to reporters after the Iran-contra scandal broke because his astrologer said that those were bad days to talk to reporters. Astrology's critics say they are sorry to see people rely like this on astrology, an outdated pseudoscience (false science), rather than depending on their own common sense and logic.

Even most astrologers frown on those who assume that the stars control every aspect of their lives. "It is not true—indeed it is most viciously false—that every moment of your present existence is controlled by the positions of the stars at your birth or at any other time," writes Charlotte MacLeod in *Astrology for Skeptics.* "All the horoscope does is to show you what conditions prevail so that you can adjust yourself to cope with them." Astrologer Marion March, founder of Aquarian Workshops in Encino, California, agrees with MacLeod. "It's a negative use of astrology to say that you have a bad horoscope and that there's nothing you can do about it," she says. "That's one of the dangers of astrology—that people use it as a scapegoat."

The positive use of astrology allows people to take advantage of favorable periods in their life, says March. She says she can look at someone's natal chart, for example, and tell him or her that the closer presence of Saturn in the next four months will allow him or her to concentrate much better than usual.

By the same token, astrologers say they can tell people when they will enter more difficult periods and times of high stress in their life. This allows them to prepare themselves and to be more resourceful, says Mary Downing, astrologer and secretary for the National Council for GeoCosmic Research. "An astrologer won't tell someone that they can't achieve anything in a stressful period," she says. "We're really tossing the responsibility back to the individual and telling them that what matters is how they decide to handle it."

March agrees that astrologers value the free choice of an individual. "Astrology is like a road map—it always leaves you the free will to take whatever road you want. The roads are mapped out so you can choose the one you want to go on," she says. "I wouldn't advise anyone to look at their chart every day to see what's going to happen in their life—that's being a slave to astrology."

A Menace to Society?

Is astrology a menace to society, as some scientists claim? Scientists like Andrew Fraknoi think that harm results when people turn to

"Astrology does offer vital information about the Self— you as an individual—and the forces that are currently influencing your life."

Astrologer Grant Lewi, *Astrology for the Millions*

"Astrology seems to work when the astrologer reading the chart is a skillful observer of human nature. The astrologer picks up quickly on what the client would like to hear and tells him whatever will make him happy."

John Mosley, *Astronomy*, February 1990

astrology to make decisions in many areas of their lives. "Throughout the world people make investments, change jobs, select their mates, and seek medical treatment on the basis of astrological forecasts," he says.

Scientists fret that one in four Americans professes a belief in astrology, according to a June 1990 Gallup poll of 1,236 Americans. While 25 percent of Americans in 1990 believed in astrology, some scientists are also happy to see that the number of believers has decreased slightly: In 1978, 29 percent of Americans said they believed in astrology, according to Gallup. Nonetheless, scientists cringe upon hearing that in addition to the believers, 74 percent of Americans admit to at least occasionally looking at their horoscope.

Disclaiming Astrology

Scientists charge that the media's promotion of astrology leads to its widespread acceptance among the public. They object that many magazines and most newspapers print daily horoscopes and occasionally the predictions of astrologers without also presenting scientists' criticisms of them. In 1990, skeptics of astrology convinced approximately thirty major newspapers in America to add disclaimers to their horoscope columns. The *Morning Advocate* in Baton Rouge, Louisiana, has a disclaimer next to its daily horoscope that says, "The horoscope, an entertainment feature, is not based on scientific fact."

"When the media's coverage of astrology leads people to base serious decisions on its predictions, then astrology is no longer a game, and can be dangerous—especially in the areas of politics and economics," says Fraknoi.

Critics of astrology point to the needless panic that wildly inaccurate astrological predictions have stirred up over the years. People have fled their homes in fear because of warnings of natural disasters ranging from floods in Europe to earthquakes in San Francisco.

Skeptics say that people who blindly believe in what an astrologer has to say are throwing their money away. Astrologers charge anywhere from a few to several hundred dollars for a horoscope, for instance. "Given a perpetually curious, often ignorant, certainly superstitious clientele to work on, vast numbers of fakers and flatterers have in the past made a more-than-adequate living out of human weakness and fear of the unknown," write Derek and Julia Parker in *The New Compleat Astrologer.*

Proof of Their Meaninglessness

Fraknoi objects not only to fake astrologers but to those who are sincere as well. Proof of their meaninglessness, he says, lies in the fact that astrologers often disagree about how to cast and read a horoscope. Different schools of astrology vary widely in their interpretations. "Any two horoscopes cast by two independent astrologers for the same individual would disagree with one another," agrees James Kaler. "The rules of astrology are so flexible that you can get almost anything you want out of it."

For example, Kaler talks about the ways some astrologers interpreted a recent "conjunction" of the planets Mars and Saturn in Capricorn. (A conjunction occurs when planets appear to move very close to each other.) "When Saturn is in Capricorn, good things will supposedly happen, and when Mars is in Capricorn, bad things will happen," he says. "So astrologers can call it any way they like. And they are likely to tell people what they want so they will come back for more readings."

To keep their customers coming back for more readings, some astrologers purposefully give them mostly positive information about their lives, say

"Those who deny the influence of the planets violate clear evidence which for educated people of sane judgment it is not suitable to contradict."

Sixteenth-century scientist Tycho Brahe, *De Disciplinus Mathematicis*

"Astrology depends very much on the ability of an astrologer to convince a person that he can give good advice, whether or not the stars have actually been consulted."

Franklyn M. Branley, *The Age of Aquarius*

critics. Astrologers go so far as to distort information to please their clients, writes Gary Jennings in *The Teenager's Realistic Guide to Astrology*. For example, some people born under the zodiac sign of Scorpio dislike the association with this poisonous creature. So some astrologers have told their clients that the constellation also represents the shape of an eagle.

Harry Shipman, astronomy professor at the University of Delaware, thinks that some astrologers, like some counselors, are skilled at picking up clues about people by listening to them closely. "Astrologers know that there are certain universal things people like to hear," he says. "College students, for instance, like to hear predictions about dating and marriage. Then an astrologer dresses a reading up with arcane symbols and all this bull about ascendants and it sounds authoritative."

Benefits of Astrology

Astrologers disagree with skeptical scientists. Astrologers claim that people can and do benefit from their science. "A good astrologer is simply a fellow human being who is making use of an immeasurably ancient discipline, and combining it with an experience of counseling and a great deal of sympathy to help his fellow creatures," write Derek and Julia Parker.

Astrologers say that people who have their natal horoscopes charted gain self-knowledge and a better ability to understand others. Astrology can also help people predict the behavior of others, says astrologer Joan Negus, director of education for the National Council for GeoCosmic Research. For instance, knowing a friend has the sign of Taurus strongly emphasized in his or her natal chart could help one deal with the classic stubbornness of this sign. "If you want a Taurus to do something, don't tell them how to do it," says Negus. "Offer a number of suggestions and let your friend pick one. Then she will have made the decision and you will get what you want without fighting."

Some parents say they use astrology as a resource in raising their children. Astrology can help parents determine issues ranging from which child needs more privacy to what toys he or she prefers. Negus says that having a child's natal chart done keeps parents from trying to force their child into the same mold as themselves. "If a parent is one to work hard and long and stick to a project, they may have trouble understanding a super-Gemini child who can't sit still for twelve seconds," she says. "But understanding what it means to be a Gemini may allow them to accept their child's

Mercury, the messenger of the gods, rules the sign Gemini the Twins. Geminis typically exhibit an intellectual bent and a talent for using language—traits associated with Mercury. Parents acquainted with their children's horoscopes are less likely to force children into roles or behavior unsuited for them, astrologers claim.

tendency to do several things at once and to spread a project out over a week."

Astrologers name other situations in which astrology is helpful. Some Wall Street brokers study the stars before trading stocks and bonds. Many use computers to track the connections they believe exist between the movement of stock and bond prices and celestial occurrences ranging from sunspot cycles to the appearance of comets and the position of the planets, says astrologer Mary Downing.

Many psychotherapists gain insight into their patients by studying their natal charts, say astrologers. "A small but increasing number of therapists are finding that astrological concepts can provide a useful framework for exploring and describing persons and situations in understandable and very human terms," write H. J. Eysenck and D. K. B. Nias in *Astrology: Science or Superstition?*

Downing says that astrologers can help with

The founders of the United States of America used astrology to determine that July 4, 1776, was the most favorable time to make their historic declaration of independence.

President Theodore Roosevelt was known to have kept an astrological chart always close at hand.

career advice. "We can't tell someone that they will be a surgeon or a concert pianist," she says. "But we can tell if a person has a capacity for precise work by looking at specific configurations in his or her natal chart."

The fact that so many prominent people have studied astrology over the centuries speaks of its worth, say astrologers. The list of believers includes leaders like Julius Caesar and Benjamin Franklin, as well as psychiatrist Carl Jung and novelist Arthur Miller. Theodore Roosevelt is said to have kept an astrological chart taped to his chessboard for reference. The founders of the United States consulted the stars for the right moment to sign the Declaration of Independence.

Despite the fact that astrology dates back many centuries and has had its share of distinguished

Charlatans who prey on the fears and superstitions of certain people have given astrology a bad reputation, according to sincere astrologers.

students, many people do not hold the field of astrology in high esteem. True, astrology can count a number of sincere and dedicated astrologers among its ranks. But the industry has also attracted an unusually high number of charlatans, or quacks, trying to take advantage of the public.

The industry's poor image springs from a variety of sources. Astrologer Marion March winces at the outrageous predictions some astrologers make in tabloid publications like the *National Enquirer.* She also objects to astrologers she sees at psychic fairs or at booths in shopping malls: Some claim to predict a person's future, much like a fortune-teller, and others promise an accurate horoscope to someone without knowing their exact time of birth. "Like gypsies, these astrologers tell people ridiculous things like they will meet a dark handsome stranger," says March. "As long as astrologers play parlor games like that, our profession won't be regarded seriously."

Incomplete Information

Popular daily horoscopes appearing in newspapers have also damaged the reputation of astrology, say many. A horoscope which only considers a person's sun sign, without any other data, is hopelessly inaccurate. Much more complete information is required to chart a person's horoscope, including the time, date, and location of birth.

It is unreasonable to suppose that the advice in a horoscope column for a Gemini, for example, could apply to every person born under that sun sign. This would include a vast category of people born under Gemini—nearly one-twelfth of the population, or approximately 400 million people around the world.

As critics point out, many people have been misinformed and cheated of their money by disreputable astrologers. Sensitive to such abuses, reputable astrologers talk about how astrology helps people when used the correct way. "Properly used, astrology teaches self-reliance and at the same time it opens up new and often unsuspected areas of life . . . which may be explored and used, and when difficulties arise, it suggests several possible approaches to a predicament, which may not have occurred to the person concerned," write Derek and Julia Parker. March also says that her clients benefit from astrology. "When my clients see their horoscope—a map of the sun and the positions of the stars and planets on the day they were born—then their interconnection with the world and its universe becomes clearer," she says.

Astrology not only allows people to feel a connection to the cosmos, say astrologers, but in a chaotic and complex world, astrology gives people a system to interpret personalities, and subsequently, a sense of inner harmony.

Is astrology more entertaining than educational, more superstitious mumbo-jumbo than scientific fact? Or is it an ancient art that allows people to achieve their fullest potential in many areas of their lives? These questions can only be answered by each individual after thoughtful exploration.

"Astrology isn't voodoo, but rather a system of world outlooks, which enables people to know themselves and their place in life, and provides them with a key to spiritual development."

Astrologer Pavel Globa, *Soviet Life*, December 1989

"Astrologers sense the deep insecurity of people who would trust them rather than themselves. . . . It lifts the weight of responsibility from the frail."

Murray L. Bob, *The Skeptical Inquirer*, Fall 1988

Epilogue

The Search Goes On

With such a confusing and contradictory mass of information about astrology, it is hard to tell if it really works. Some astrologers have made surprisingly accurate predictions. Other astrologers, like those in tabloid newspapers, routinely make predictions that are so general as to be meaningless.

If the past is any indication, it seems unlikely that the truth about astrology will be known in the near future—if ever. Most likely, scientists will continue to hold the view of Lawrence Jerome, author of *Astrology Disproved*. "Astrology, in the way it operates and in the way characteristics of the various celestial objects are assigned to people and events, is a system of magic," he writes. "No amount of rhetoric, false claims, or statistical studies can alter that fact. Magic astrology was born, and magic it will remain."

But scientists like Andrew Fraknoi admit that no amount of scientific evidence refuting astrology will affect its popularity for some people. "Even today, despite so much effort at science education, astrology's appeal for many people has not diminished," he says. "For them, thinking of Venus as a cloud-covered desert world as hot as an oven is far less attractive than seeing it as an aid in deciding whom to marry."

Whether or not scientists prove or refute the tenets of astrology, this age-old art will always have its fol-

lowers. The fact that astrology has persevered shows that it serves a purpose for many people. "We keep rediscovering the ancient lore because we need it," writes Charlotte MacLeod in *Astrology for Skeptics.* "We have to learn where we fit into the ecology of time and space. We require information on how to adjust not only to the familiar world of things but to the vaster worlds of mind and spirit. We know there's a sound idea under the incense and the nonsense."

Suffice it to say that interest in astrology is likely to survive as long as the planets swirl around the sun and meteors shower the skies.

Debate about the influence of the stars on human lives will doubtless continue for as long as the stars dot the heavens.

Appendix A

Casting a Simple Horoscope

The horoscope columns in most magazines and newspapers are based exclusively on a person's sun sign. But a practicing astrologer who draws up a natal chart considers not just a person's sun sign, but the position of many other planets and stars as well. For example, astrologers think that having the sun and ascendant sign in the same constellation enhances the effect of that sign. A man for whom both his sun and ascendant are Pisces, for instance, would share more of the characteristics of Pisces than if his sun were in Pisces and his ascendant in a different zodiac sign.

The time of the month a person is born can also affect how a sun sign is interpreted. Those born on the cusp, or the borderline between two signs, are said to have some of the traits of both signs. For instance, if someone was born on May 20, the next-to-last day of Taurus, then they would share some qualities of Gemini, which begins on May 22.

Characteristics of Sun Signs

Many horoscopes deal with how other planets enhance or diminish the effect of a person's sun sign. So it is useful to know the basic characteristics of the twelve sun signs before attempting to cast a horoscope. (The dates here follow the traditional astrological calendar.)

Aries the Ram
March 21-April 20
Symbol: ♈

This first sign of the zodiac has the ram for its symbol. Because rams often fight, ancient astrologers said that Aries was ruled by Mars, the planet named after the Roman god of war.

Like rams, Ariens are said to be stubborn, daring, and forceful. Perpetually in motion, they love to be constantly involved in activities and to lead other people. Ariens are endlessly enthusiastic and curious and pursue many goals with determination. But they have a tendency to be reckless, headstrong, and quick-tempered. While they like to have power over others, they demand freedom for themselves and often defy authority.

Ariens make clever conversationalists and relish being the center of attention. They are accident-prone and tend to be careless about their health.

Taurus the Bull
April 21-May 21
Symbol: ♉

Taureans are ruled by the planet Venus, named after the Roman goddess of beauty and love. Warm and affectionate, they are said to admire art and beauty. Like the bull they are named after, Taureans are stubborn, steady, and strong. And like Ariens, they push toward their goals with great determination.

Taureans are practical, down-to-earth, and honest people. They love luxury but will not spend too much money because they hate to be in debt. Since Taureans love to eat, drink, and go to parties, they often gain too much weight.

While Taureans do not like to be told what to do, they are not pushy or aggressive. With their love of home and the family, and their agreeable temperaments, they make excellent parents.

Gemini the Twins
May 22-June 21
Symbol: ♊

People born under Gemini are ruled by the planet Mercury, named after the Roman god who carried messages for the gods. This is why Gemini people are known for being quick and athletic. They are also said to have two personalities, since their sign is the twins. Gemini people can be talkative and playful one day and sarcastic and temperamental the next.

Said to lead a double life, many Gemini people are happiest when they have two jobs and hobbies at the same time. Charming and energetic, they love to travel and meet new people. But they are also impatient and have difficulty concentrating on one thing at a time. They tend to have trouble sleeping and become easily fatigued.

Cancer the Crab
June 22-July 22
Symbol: ♋

Cancers are ruled by the moon. Since the moon causes tides to change, Cancers are also said to like change. Symbolized by the crab, they prefer to stay at home, like staying in a shell. They love comfort and warmth. Emotional and sentimental, they keep scrapbooks and souvenirs of all kinds.

Emotional Cancers need to feel loved. They are also very sensitive to criticism. Cancers demand loyalty from their friends. They have great pride and are considered the most patriotic of all the signs.

Leo the Lion
July 23-August 23
Symbol: ♌

Since they are ruled by the sun, Leos are bright and loving. Like the lion they are named after, proud Leos hold their heads high. Particularly outgoing, they love to be the center of attention. Leos crave excitement and dislike the routine and ordinary.

They are self-confident to the point of being boastful. Loving sports, Leos play to win. They are generous with their time and love to teach and explain to others. But a Leo's high level of ambition leaves him or her very frustrated with failure.

Virgo the Virgin
August 24-September 23
Symbol: ♍

Perfectionist Virgos are methodical, fussy, and practical. With their love of order, they are always cleaning and tidying up. Unlike Aries and Leo, the reserved and gentle Virgo does not mind routine, detailed work. They also prefer to work alone and do not seek leadership positions.

Like Mercury, the god that gave their ruling planet its name, Virgos love to travel. More intellectual than emotional, they often hurt other people with their sharp tongues. In an emergency, logical Virgos do not panic; they make sound decisions.

Libra the Scales
September 24-October 23
Symbol: ♎

Peaceloving, artistic Librans are ruled by Venus, named after the god of love and beauty.

They love the arts and also want to have a rich social life. Like Virgos, they are tidy perfectionists who pay attention to detail.

Named after weighing scales, Librans weigh each side of an issue very carefully before making a decision. Some would say that they take too long to make up their minds, but Librans are also known to be fair and interested in justice. Unaggressive people, they strive for harmony in their lives.

Scorpio the Scorpion
October 24-November 22
Symbol: ♏

Scorpios are ruled by the planets Mars, named after the Roman god of war, and Pluto, named after the Greek god of the underworld. Scorpios are more powerful, intense, and magnetic than any other sign and are drawn to mystery and secrets. Scorpios' strong emotions cause them to be passionate and loyal to friends. But they can also be vengeful, quick-tempered, and jealous.

Scorpios are critical of others but dislike being criticized themselves. Hating to give in to others' viewpoints, they can argue endlessly. This bullheadedness also means that Scorpios usually succeed at whatever they attempt, no matter how impossible it may seem.

Sagittarius the Archer
November 23-December 21
Symbol: ♐

Sagittarians are ruled by Jupiter, known to the Romans as the king of the gods. Like the archer's arrow, Sagittarians are said to be direct and sometimes brutally honest. They also rely on their instincts and intuitions, much like Librans.

Sagittarians love to travel and explore and are often philosophical. Frequently involved in sports and a number of activities, they are busy people to catch up with. Because of their impulsiveness, they sometimes make decisions too quickly.

Capricorn the Goat
December 22-January 20
Symbol: ♑

Like the mountain goat they were named after, Capricorns are surefooted and steady. Their ambition causes them to be social climbers and pursuers of material success. Saturn, named after the Roman god, gives them leadership qualities.

Unsentimental Capricorns tend to be practical, conservative, and cautious. They can also be stubborn. Because they are not high-spirited, Capricorns are prone to depression, which may lead to drinking or taking drugs.

Aquarius the Water Carrier
January 21-February 19
Symbol: ♒

Named after the water bearer who served the gods, Aquarians are generous, caring people. Because of the unusual tilt of their ruling planet Uranus, Aquarians are also said to be unique and creative. They are broad-visioned and open-minded internationalists and humanitarians. Despite their soft-spokenness, Aquarians have great leadership potential.

Even-tempered Aquarians can solve problems logically but also possess a degree of imagination. More idealistic than argumentative, they dislike debate and are not ones to hold out for their point of view.

Pisces the Fish
February 20-March 20
Symbol: ♓

The planet Neptune, who presides over the sea, rules Pisces. Pisceans are said to swim with the current, rather than against it. And like the fish that live in the depths of the ocean, Pisceans seem a little unreachable and hard to know. But their sympathy and generosity toward others make them very understanding friends.

Pisceans lack social and career ambition. Gentle and dreamy, they are drawn to the artistic fields. Because Pisceans lack self-confidence and a sense of practicality, they have a hard time getting things done. Like Capricorns, their melancholia makes them susceptible to drug and alcohol abuse.

Casting a Horoscope

In casting a horoscope or natal chart, astrologers draw a map of the sky for a person's date of birth. For an accurate map, astrologers say they need to know the location and exact time of birth.

For the purposes of determining your ascendant sign now, consult appendix B. It lists ascendant signs—the sign of the zodiac that was rising on the eastern horizon at the time of one's birth—for every hour for every four days throughout the year. If your birthday falls in between the four days, choose the date closer to your birthday.

Find your moon sign by consulting appendix C. Look for your year and month of birth on the table. You will find a moon sign for every two days. To calculate your moon sign, find the closest day to your birthday on the chart.

Once you know both your moon and ascendant signs, you can begin to label your horoscope. Look at the following illustration. It shows a 360-degree circle with twelve pie-shaped compartments and another circle around its rim. Note that the pie pieces—the houses—are numbered in a counterclockwise direction, beginning at the nine o'clock position. The dividing lines between the houses are called cusps.

Now fill in the signs of the zodiac according to your birthdate. Let's take the example of Margaret, who was born at 10:00 A.M. on November 19, 1980, in Chicago. Her sun sign is Scorpio since she was born between October 24

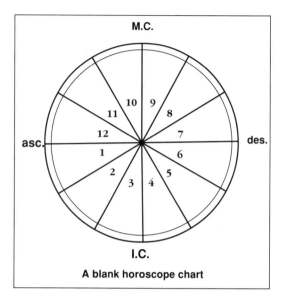

A blank horoscope chart

and November 22. According to the simplified moon table (Appendix C), the moon was in Aries on November 19, 1980.

Appendix B shows that the ascendant sign for 10:00 A.M. is Capricorn.

Fill in Capricorn, her ascendant, in the outer circle at the cusp of the first house, at the nine o'clock position. Then label the circle with the remaining signs of the zodiac in calendar order. After Capricorn in the first house, the second house would be Aquarius, the third house Pisces, and so forth.

Margaret's descendant sign, the sign that was setting on the western horizon when she was born, is Cancer; it is written across from the ascendant on the right side of the circle, at the seventh house cusp. At the top is Libra, the midheaven or medium coeli (M.C.), at the tenth house cusp. At the bottom, at six o'clock, is her nadir or imum coeli (I.C.), at the fourth house cusp. To an astrologer, each of these points is important. For simplicity, we will not get into their functions here.

Astrologers would also place all ten planets

(the eight planets in our solar system, excluding earth, plus the sun and the moon) on the chart. For the purpose of simplicity, the only planets we will draw on Margaret's chart are the sun and moon. Draw the symbol for the sun ☉ in the house labeled Scorpio. Since you know Margaret's moon sign is Aries, draw a moon symbol ☽ in the house labeled Aries.

You can complete your own chart in the same manner. Begin by placing your ascendant on the cusp of the first house and continuing around the circle as you did with Margaret's.

With the completed horoscope, an astrologer can interpret the effect of the zodiac signs in each house. The twelve houses each represent a different feature of life. Here is a definition of the houses and a very brief and simplified interpretation of what the houses mean in Margaret's chart:

1. House of self:

How one appears to the outside world, including personality, health, and physical appearance.

Margaret has Capricorn in her first house.

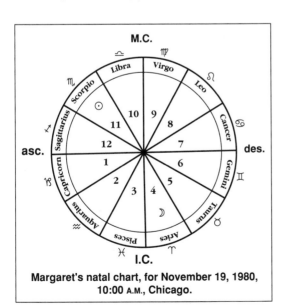

Margaret's natal chart, for November 19, 1980, 10:00 A.M., Chicago.

This means that she will have a conservative and structured approach to life. Because Capricorns work hard and are ambitious, Margaret will strive to overcome difficulties in her career and in all areas of her life.

2. House of wealth:

Money and possessions and attitudes about them.

The generous sign of Aquarius in this house means that Margaret will lend money to friends in need. She is also not likely to want to make money just for money's sake, since Aquarius exerts a carefree, broad-minded influence.

3. House of communications:

Relationships with brothers and sisters, neighbors, and groups; all kinds of communications with others; short travel.

Pisces in the third house indicates that Margaret will be receptive and sympathetic in her communications with others. If she works in an office, people there might have a tendency to share their problems with Margaret.

4. House of home:

Includes the environment one creates around oneself and family life, especially parents.

Having impulsive and reckless Aries in this house means that Margaret will create an atmosphere of energy and boldness at home but will have to be careful not to upset its harmony. She will also tend to defy authority and to be possessive of people she loves.

Having the moon in this house reinforces Margaret's impulsiveness. She will have to use her strong will power to cultivate patience, tolerance, and moderation to create a healthy balance in her life.

5. House of romance:

Also rules the creativity, children, and pleasurable activities such as leisure, sports, and gambling.

A Taurean influence here means that Margaret will be warm and affectionate in her love life. But as an earth sign, she will not necessarily be romantic. This sign also means that Margaret will make an excellent parent and will center her interests on her children.

6. House of health:

Includes work, and relationships with employees and with grandparents, uncles, and aunts.

Gemini in the sixth house means that Margaret will need work that gives her an outlet for her considerable creative energies. As a typical Gemini, she might want to work two jobs at once. Margaret may be difficult to work for, since she will tend to disagree and to communicate in so many different ways.

7. House of marriage:

Desire and attitude toward marriage and other personal and professional relationships.

Margaret will be possessive, nurturing, and protective of her spouse with the influence of Cancer here. She will demand loyalty from her friends and business associates.

8. House of change:

The process of life, including reincarnation. (This house used to be called the house of death.) Also covers business, divorces, and wills.

Leo in the eighth house shows that Margaret will handle change with self-confidence and bravery. But she will also have difficulty accepting failure when change does not work out the way she likes.

9. House of travel:

Long-distance travel and intellectual interests such as higher education, religion, and philosophy.

With Virgo in this house, Margaret is likely to plan her trips to the minute, with the methodi-

cal, organized qualities of a Virgo. The meticulous and serious Virgo nature also bodes well for Margaret if she pursues higher education; she will make an excellent student.

10. House of career:

Also identity in the community and relationships with father and employers.

Since Librans are often go-betweens or referees, Margaret may choose work where she can help people communicate, such as being a diplomat or television anchorperson. Libra is also in Margaret's cusp of the mid-heaven, which affects her public life and standing in the community. Since Librans are peacemakers, Margaret may repress her own personality in order to be at harmony with the world.

11. House of friends:

Social life, including friends and clubs one joins. Also hopes, wishes, and political activity.

Because of the influence of Scorpio and the sun, Margaret's friends will find her a loyal and passionate companion who may be jealous and suspicious at times. In any organizations she belongs to, Margaret will want to take control.

12. House of secrets:

The need to seclude oneself and to serve others. Governs the subconscious mind and all aspects of seclusion, such as monasteries, prisons, and hospitals.

Having Sagittarius in the twelfth house is a positive sign for Margaret. Since Sagittarius exerts an open and honest influence, she is unlikely to be threatened by secret enemies.

This was a very brief and simplified interpretation of Margaret's natal chart.

In addition to interpreting the signs of the zodiac in each house, professional astrologers note the exact positions of the planets. Then they relate how signs, houses, and heavenly bodies all interact together. For example, astrologers pay particular attention to heavenly bodies located near the ascendant, descendant, and mid-heaven. A professional astrologer would give a much more detailed reading. But the exercise you just completed can give you an idea of whether you might like to have a more detailed and accurate horoscope cast.

Appendix B

Simplified Ascendant Sign Table

1 = ♈ (Aries)   4 = ♋ (Cancer)   7 = ♎ (Libra)   10 = ♑ (Capricorn)
2 = ♉ (Taurus)   5 = ♌ (Leo)   8 = ♏ (Scorpio)   11 = ♒ (Aquarius)
3 = ♊ (Gemini)   6 = ♍ (Virgo)   9 = ♐ (Sagittarius) 12 = ♓ (Pisces)

Source: Gary Jennings, *The Teenager's Realistic Guide to Astrology.*

TIME

	AM										NOON						PM						Midn't.
DATE	1	2	3	4	5	6	7	8	9	10	11	12	1	2	3	4	5	6	7	8	9	10	11	12
January 1	7	8	8	8	9	9	10	10	11	11	12	1	2	3	3	4	4	4	5	5	6	6	6	7
January 5	7	8	8	8	9	9	10	10	11	12	12	1	2	3	3	4	4	5	5	5	6	6	7	7
January 9	7	8	8	9	9	9	10	10	11	12	1	2	2	3	3	4	4	5	5	5	6	6	6	7
January 13	7	8	8	9	9	10	10	11	11	12	1	2	2	3	3	4	4	5	5	6	6	6	7	7
January 17	8	8	8	9	9	10	10	11	11	12	1	2	3	3	4	4	4	5	5	6	6	6	7	7
January 21	8	8	8	9	9	10	10	11	12	12	1	2	3	3	4	4	4	5	5	6	6	6	7	7
January 25	8	8	9	9	9	10	10	11	12	1	2	2	3	3	4	4	5	5	5	6	6	7	7	7
January 29	8	8	9	9	10	10	11	11	12	1	2	2	3	4	4	4	5	5	6	6	6	7	7	8
February 2	8	8	9	9	10	10	11	12	12	1	2	3	3	4	4	4	5	5	6	6	6	7	7	8
February 6	8	8	9	9	10	10	11	12	1	1	2	3	3	4	4	5	5	5	6	6	7	7	7	8
February 10	8	9	9	9	10	10	11	12	1	2	2	3	3	4	4	5	5	5	6	6	7	7	7	8
February 14	8	9	9	10	10	11	11	12	1	2	2	3	4	4	4	5	5	6	6	6	7	7	8	8
February 18	8	9	9	10	10	11	12	12	1	2	3	3	4	4	4	5	5	6	6	6	7	7	8	8
February 22	9	9	9	10	10	11	12	1	1	2	3	3	4	4	5	5	5	6	6	7	7	7	8	8
February 26	9	9	9	10	11	11	12	1	2	2	3	3	4	4	5	5	5	6	6	7	7	7	8	8
March 2	9	9	10	10	11	11	12	1	2	3	3	4	4	4	5	5	6	6	6	7	7	8	8	8
March 6	9	9	10	10	11	12	12	1	2	3	3	4	4	5	5	5	6	6	6	7	7	8	8	8
March 10	9	9	10	10	11	12	1	2	2	3	3	4	4	5	5	5	6	6	7	7	7	8	8	9
March 14	9	10	10	11	11	12	1	2	2	3	3	4	4	5	5	6	6	6	7	7	7	8	8	9
March 18	9	10	10	11	11	12	1	2	3	3	4	4	4	5	5	6	6	6	7	7	8	8	8	9
March 22	9	10	10	11	12	1	1	2	3	3	4	4	5	5	5	6	6	7	7	7	8	8	9	9
March 26	9	10	10	11	12	1	2	2	3	3	4	4	5	5	5	6	6	7	7	7	8	8	9	9
March 30	10	10	11	11	12	1	2	2	3	4	4	4	5	5	6	6	6	7	7	8	8	9	9	9
April 3	10	10	11	12	12	1	2	3	3	4	4	4	5	5	6	6	6	7	7	8	8	9	9	9
April 7	10	10	11	12	1	1	2	3	3	4	4	5	5	5	6	6	7	7	7	8	8	9	9	9
April 10	10	10	11	12	1	2	2	3	3	4	4	5	5	5	6	6	7	7	7	8	8	9	9	9
April 14	10	11	11	12	1	2	2	3	3	4	4	5	5	6	6	6	7	7	8	8	8	9	9	10
April 18	10	11	12	12	1	2	3	3	4	4	4	5	5	6	6	6	7	7	8	8	8	9	9	10
April 22	10	11	12	1	1	2	3	3	4	4	5	5	5	6	6	7	7	7	8	8	9	9	9	10
April 26	10	11	12	1	2	2	3	3	4	4	5	5	5	6	6	7	7	7	8	8	9	9	9	10

DATE	AM											NOON		PM										Midn't.
	1	2	3	4	5	6	7	8	9	10	11	12	1	2	3	4	5	6	7	8	9	10	11	12
April 30	11	11	12	1	2	2	3	4	4	4	5	5	6	6	6	7	7	8	8	8	9	9	10	10
May 4	11	12	12	1	2	3	3	4	4	4	5	5	6	6	6	7	7	8	8	8	9	9	10	10
May 8	11	12	1	1	2	3	3	4	4	5	5	5	6	6	7	7	7	8	8	9	9	9	10	10
May 12	11	12	1	2	2	3	3	4	4	5	5	5	6	6	7	7	7	8	8	9	9	9	10	11
May 16	11	12	1	2	3	3	4	4	4	5	5	6	6	6	7	7	8	8	8	9	9	10	10	11
May 20	12	12	1	2	3	3	4	4	5	5	5	6	6	6	7	7	8	8	8	9	9	10	10	11
May 24	12	1	1	2	3	3	4	4	5	5	5	6	6	7	7	7	8	8	9	9	9	10	10	11
May 28	12	1	2	2	3	3	4	4	5	5	5	6	6	7	7	7	8	8	9	9	9	10	11	11
June 1	12	1	2	3	3	4	4	4	5	5	6	6	6	7	7	8	8	8	9	9	10	10	11	11
June 5	12	1	2	3	3	4	4	5	5	5	6	6	6	7	7	8	8	8	9	9	10	10	11	12
June 9	1	1	2	3	3	4	4	5	5	5	6	6	7	7	7	8	8	9	9	9	10	10	11	12
June 13	1	2	2	3	3	4	4	5	5	5	6	6	7	7	7	8	8	9	9	9	10	11	11	12
June 17	1	2	3	3	4	4	4	5	5	6	6	6	7	7	8	8	8	9	9	10	10	11	11	12
June 21	1	2	3	3	4	4	5	5	5	6	6	6	7	7	8	8	8	9	9	10	10	11	12	12
June 25	2	2	3	3	4	4	5	5	5	6	6	7	7	7	8	8	9	9	9	10	10	11	12	1
June 29	2	2	3	3	4	4	5	5	6	6	6	7	7	7	8	8	9	9	10	10	11	11	12	1
July 3	2	3	3	4	4	4	5	5	6	6	6	7	7	8	8	8	9	9	10	10	11	11	12	1
July 7	2	3	3	4	4	5	5	5	6	6	6	7	7	8	8	8	9	9	10	10	11	12	1	1
July 11	2	3	3	4	4	5	5	5	6	6	7	7	7	8	8	9	9	9	10	10	11	12	1	2
July 14	2	3	3	4	4	5	5	5	6	6	7	7	7	8	8	9	9	10	10	11	11	12	1	2
July 18	3	3	4	4	4	5	5	6	6	6	7	7	8	8	8	9	9	10	10	11	11	12	1	2
July 22	3	3	4	4	5	5	5	6	6	6	7	7	8	8	8	9	9	10	10	11	12	12	1	2
July 26	3	3	4	4	5	5	5	6	6	6	7	7	8	8	9	9	9	10	10	11	12	1	2	2
July 30	3	3	4	4	5	5	6	6	6	7	7	7	8	8	9	9	10	10	11	11	12	1	2	2
August 3	3	4	4	4	5	5	6	6	6	7	7	8	8	8	9	9	10	10	11	11	12	1	2	3
August 7	3	4	4	5	5	5	6	6	7	7	7	8	8	8	9	9	10	10	11	12	1	1	2	3
August 11	3	4	4	5	5	5	6	6	7	7	7	8	8	9	9	9	10	10	11	12	1	2	2	3
August 15	4	4	4	5	5	6	6	6	7	7	8	8	8	9	9	10	10	11	11	12	1	2	2	3
August 19	4	4	4	5	5	6	6	6	7	7	8	8	8	9	9	10	10	11	12	12	1	2	3	3
August 23	4	4	5	5	5	6	6	7	7	7	8	8	9	9	9	10	10	11	12	1	1	2	3	3
August 27	4	4	5	5	5	6	6	7	7	7	8	8	9	9	9	10	10	11	12	1	2	2	3	3
August 31	4	4	5	5	6	6	6	7	7	8	8	8	9	9	10	10	11	11	12	1	2	3	3	4
September 4	4	4	5	5	6	6	6	7	7	8	8	8	9	9	10	10	11	12	12	1	2	3	3	4
September 8	4	5	5	5	6	6	7	7	7	8	8	9	9	9	10	10	11	12	1	1	2	3	3	4
September 12	4	5	5	5	6	6	7	7	7	8	8	9	9	9	10	10	11	12	1	2	2	3	3	4
September 16	4	5	5	6	6	6	7	7	8	8	8	9	9	10	10	11	11	12	1	2	3	3	4	4
September 20	5	5	5	6	6	6	7	7	8	8	8	9	9	10	10	11	12	12	1	2	3	3	4	4
September 24	5	5	5	6	6	7	7	7	8	8	9	9	10	10	11	11	12	1	2	2	3	3	4	4
September 28	5	5	5	6	6	7	7	7	8	8	9	9	10	10	11	11	12	1	2	2	3	3	4	4
October 2	5	5	6	6	6	7	7	8	8	8	9	9	10	10	11	11	12	1	2	3	3	4	4	4
October 6	5	5	6	6	6	7	7	8	8	8	9	9	10	10	11	12	1	1	2	3	3	4	4	5
October 10	5	5	6	6	7	7	7	8	8	9	9	9	10	10	11	12	1	2	2	3	3	4	4	5
October 14	5	6	6	6	7	7	7	8	8	9	9	10	10	11	11	12	1	2	2	3	3	4	4	5
October 18	5	6	6	7	7	7	8	8	8	9	9	10	10	11	11	12	1	2	3	3	4	4	5	5
October 22	5	6	6	7	7	7	8	8	9	9	9	10	10	11	12	1	1	2	3	3	4	4	5	5
October 26	5	6	6	7	7	7	8	8	9	9	9	10	10	11	12	1	2	2	3	3	4	4	5	5
October 30	6	6	6	7	7	8	8	8	9	9	10	10	11	11	12	1	2	2	3	4	4	4	5	5
November 3	6	6	6	7	7	8	8	8	9	9	10	10	11	12	1	2	2	3	3	4	4	4	5	5
November 7	6	6	7	7	7	8	8	9	9	9	10	10	11	12	1	1	2	3	3	4	4	5	5	5
November 11	6	6	7	7	7	8	8	9	9	9	10	10	11	11	12	1	2	2	3	3	4	4	5	5
November 15	6	6	7	7	8	8	8	9	9	10	10	11	11	12	1	2	3	3	4	4	4	5	5	6
November 19	6	6	7	7	8	8	8	9	9	10	10	11	12	12	1	2	3	3	4	4	5	5	5	6
November 23	6	7	7	7	8	8	9	9	9	10	10	11	12	1	1	2	3	3	4	4	5	5	5	6
November 27	6	7	7	7	8	8	9	9	9	10	11	11	12	1	2	2	3	3	4	4	5	5	5	6
December 1	6	7	7	8	8	8	9	9	10	10	11	11	12	1	2	3	3	4	4	4	5	5	6	6
December 5	6	7	7	8	8	8	9	9	10	10	11	12	12	1	2	3	3	4	4	4	5	5	6	6
December 9	7	7	7	8	8	9	9	9	10	10	11	12	1	2	2	3	3	4	4	5	5	6	6	6
December 13	7	7	7	8	8	9	9	9	10	11	11	12	1	2	2	3	3	4	4	5	5	6	6	6
December 18	7	7	8	8	8	9	9	10	10	11	11	12	1	2	3	3	4	4	5	5	5	6	6	6
December 23	7	7	8	8	9	9	9	10	10	11	12	1	1	2	3	3	4	4	5	5	5	6	6	7
December 28	7	7	8	8	9	9	9	10	11	11	12	1	2	2	3	3	4	4	5	5	6	6	6	7

Appendix C

Moon Signs, Simplified

1 = ♈ (Aries)   4 = ♋ (Cancer)   7 = ♎ (Libra)   10 = ♑ (Capricorn)
2 = ♉ (Taurus)   5 = ♌ (Leo)   8 = ♏ (Scorpio)   11 = ♒ (Aquarius)
3 = ♊ (Gemini)   6 = ♍ (Virgo)   9 = ♐ (Sagittarius)   12 = ♓ (Pisces)

Source: *The Ephemeris of the Moon, 1800-2000 Inclusive.* Compiled by Hugh MacCraig.

1975

DATE	Ja	Fe	Mr	Ap	Ma	Jn	Jl	Ag	Se	Oc	Nv	De
1	6	7	8	9	10	12	1	2	4	5	7	8
3	7	8	9	10	11	1	2	3	5	6	8	9
5	7	9	9	11	12	1	3	4	6	7	9	10
7	8	10	10	12	1	2	3	5	7	8	10	11
9	9	11	11	1	2	3	4	6	8	9	11	12
11	10	12	12	1	2	4	5	7	9	10	12	1
13	11	12	1	2	3	5	6	8	10	11	12	1
15	12	1	1	3	4	6	7	9	11	12	1	2
17	12	2	2	4	5	7	8	10	11	12	2	3
19	1	3	3	5	6	8	9	11	12	1	3	4
21	2	4	4	6	7	9	10	12	1	2	4	5
23	3	5	5	7	8	10	11	12	2	3	5	6
25	4	6	6	8	9	11	12	1	3	4	5	7
27	5	7	7	9	10	11	12	2	3	5	6	8
29	6		8	10	11	12	1	3	4	6	7	9
31	7		9		12		2	4		7		10

1976

DATE	Ja	Fe	Mr	Ap	Ma	Jn	Jl	Ag	Se	Oc	Nv	De
1	10	12	12	2	3	4	6	7	9	10	12	1
3	11	12	1	3	4	5	7	8	10	11	1	2
5	12	1	2	3	5	6	8	9	11	12	2	3
7	1	2	3	4	5	7	8	10	12	1	2	3
9	1	3	3	5	6	8	9	11	1	2	3	4
11	2	4	4	6	7	9	10	12	1	3	4	5
13	3	5	5	7	8	10	11	1	2	3	5	6
15	4	6	6	8	9	11	12	2	3	4	6	7
17	5	7	7	9	10	12	1	2	4	5	7	8
19	6	7	8	10	11	1	2	3	5	6	8	9
21	7	8	9	11	12	1	2	4	6	7	9	10
23	8	9	10	12	1	2	3	5	7	8	10	11
25	9	10	11	12	2	3	4	6	8	9	11	12
27	9	11	12	1	2	4	5	7	9	10	11	1
29	10	12	1	2	3	5	6	8	10	11	12	1
31	11		1		4		7	9		12		2

1977

DATE	Ja	Fe	Mr	Ap	Ma	Jn	Jl	Ag	Se	Oc	Nv	De
1	3	4	4	6	7	9	10	12	1	3	4	5
3	3	5	5	7	8	10	11	1	2	3	5	6
5	4	6	6	8	9	11	12	2	3	4	6	7
7	5	7	7	9	10	12	1	2	4	5	7	8
9	6	8	8	10	11	1	2	3	5	6	7	9
11	7	9	9	11	12	1	3	4	6	7	8	10
13	8	10	10	12	1	2	3	5	6	8	9	11
15	9	11	11	12	2	3	4	6	7	9	10	12
17	10	11	12	1	2	4	5	7	8	10	11	12
19	11	12	1	2	3	5	6	8	9	11	12	1
21	12	1	1	3	4	5	7	8	10	11	1	2
23	12	2	2	4	5	6	8	9	11	12	2	3
25	1	3	3	4	6	7	9	10	12	1	3	4
27	2	4	4	5	6	8	10	11	1	2	4	5
29	3		5	6	7	9	11	12	2	3	4	6
31	4		5		8		11	1		4		6

1978

DATE	Ja	Fe	Mr	Ap	Ma	Jn	Jl	Ag	Se	Oc	Nv	De
1	7	8	9	10	12	1	3	4	6	7	8	10
3	8	9	10	11	1	2	3	5	6	8	9	11
5	9	10	11	12	2	3	4	6	7	8	10	12
7	10	11	12	1	2	4	5	6	8	9	11	12
9	11	12	1	2	3	5	6	7	9	10	12	1
11	12	1	1	3	4	5	7	8	10	11	1	2
13	12	2	2	4	5	6	7	9	11	12	2	3
15	1	3	3	5	6	7	8	10	12	1	3	4
17	2	4	4	5	6	8	9	11	1	2	4	5
19	3	4	5	6	7	9	10	12	2	3	4	5
21	4	5	5	7	8	10	11	1	3	4	5	6
23	4	6	6	8	9	11	12	2	3	4	6	7
25	5	7	7	9	10	12	1	3	4	5	7	8
27	6	8	8	10	11	1	2	4	5	6	8	9
29	7		9	11	12	2	3	4	6	7	9	10
31	8		10		1		4	5		8		11

1979

DATE	Ja	Fe	Mr	Ap	Ma	Jn	Jl	Ag	Se	Oc	Nv	De
1	11	1	1	3	4	6	7	8	10	11	1	2
3	12	2	2	4	5	6	7	9	11	12	2	3
5	1	3	3	5	6	7	8	10	12	1	3	4
7	2	4	4	5	6	8	9	11	1	2	4	5
9	3	4	5	6	7	9	10	12	2	3	4	6
11	4	5	5	7	8	10	11	1	3	4	5	6
13	5	6	6	8	9	11	12	2	3	5	6	7
15	5	7	7	9	10	12	1	3	4	5	7	8
17	6	8	8	10	11	1	2	4	5	6	8	9
19	7	9	9	11	12	2	3	4	6	7	9	10
21	8	9	10	12	1	3	4	5	7	8	9	11
23	9	10	11	12	2	3	4	6	7	9	10	12
25	10	11	12	1	3	4	5	7	8	10	11	1
27	11	12	1	2	4	5	6	8	9	10	12	1
29	12		2	3	4	6	7	8	10	11	1	2
31	1		3		5		8	9		12		3

1980

DATE	Ja	Fe	Mr	Ap	Ma	Jn	Jl	Ag	Se	Oc	Nv	De
1	4	5	6	7	9	10	11	1	3	4	6	7
3	5	6	7	8	9	11	12	2	4	5	7	8
5	5	7	8	9	10	12	1	3	5	6	7	8
7	6	8	8	10	11	1	2	4	5	7	8	9
9	7	8	9	11	12	2	3	5	6	7	9	10
11	8	9	10	12	1	3	4	6	8	9	10	11
13	9	10	11	1	2	4	5	6	8	9	11	12
15	9	11	12	2	3	5	6	7	9	10	11	1
17	10	12	1	3	4	5	7	8	10	11	12	2
19	11	1	2	4	5	6	7	9	10	12	1	3
21	12	2	3	5	6	7	8	10	11	1	2	4
23	1	3	4	5	6	8	9	11	12	2	3	5
25	2	4	5	6	7	9	10	12	1	3	4	5
27	3	5	5	7	8	10	11	1	2	4	5	6
29	4	6	6	8	9	10	12	2	3	4	6	7
31	5		7		10		1	2		5		8

1981

DATE	Ja	Fe	Mr	Ap	Ma	Jn	Jl	Ag	Se	Oc	Nv	De
1	8	10	10	12	1	3	4	6	7	8	10	11
3	9	11	11	1	2	4	5	6	8	9	10	12
5	10	12	12	2	3	5	6	7	9	10	11	1
7	11	12	1	3	4	5	7	8	10	11	12	1
9	12	1	2	4	5	6	7	9	10	11	1	2
11	1	2	3	4	6	7	8	10	11	12	2	3
13	1	3	4	5	6	8	9	11	12	1	3	4
15	2	4	5	6	7	9	10	11	1	2	4	5
17	3	5	5	7	8	10	11	12	2	3	5	6
19	4	6	6	8	9	10	12	1	3	4	6	7
21	5	7	7	9	10	11	12	2	4	5	7	8
23	6	8	8	9	10	12	1	3	5	6	8	9
25	7	8	9	10	11	1	2	4	6	7	8	9
27	8	9	9	11	12	2	3	5	7	8	9	10
29	8		10	12	1	3	4	6	7	9	10	11
31	9		11		2		5	7		9		12

1982

DATE	Ja	Fe	Mr	Ap	Ma	Jn	Jl	Ag	Se	Oc	Nv	De
1	12	2	2	4	6	7	8	10	11	12	2	3
3	1	3	3	5	6	8	9	11	12	1	3	4
5	2	4	4	6	7	9	10	11	1	2	4	5
7	3	5	5	7	8	10	11	12	2	3	5	6
9	4	6	6	8	9	10	11	1	3	4	6	7
11	5	7	7	9	10	11	12	2	4	5	7	8
13	6	8	8	9	10	12	1	3	5	6	8	9
15	7	8	9	10	11	1	2	4	6	7	8	10
17	8	9	10	11	12	2	3	5	7	8	9	10
19	9	10	10	12	1	3	4	6	7	9	10	11
21	9	11	11	1	2	4	5	7	8	9	11	12
23	10	12	12	2	3	5	6	8	9	10	12	1
25	11	1	1	3	4	6	7	8	10	11	12	2
27	12	2	2	4	5	7	8	9	11	12	1	3
29	1		3	5	6	7	9	10	11	1	2	4
31	2		4		7		9	11		2		5

1983

DATE	Ja	Fe	Mr	Ap	Ma	Jn	Jl	Ag	Se	Oc	Nv	De
1	5	7	7	9	10	11	12	2	3	5	7	8
3	6	8	8	9	11	12	1	3	4	6	7	9
5	7	8	9	10	11	1	2	4	5	7	8	10
7	8	9	10	11	12	2	3	5	6	8	9	10
9	8	10	10	12	1	3	4	6	7	9	10	11
11	9	11	11	1	2	4	5	7	8	9	11	12
13	10	12	12	2	3	5	6	8	9	10	12	1
15	11	1	1	2	4	6	7	8	10	11	12	2
17	12	1	2	3	5	6	8	9	11	12	1	2
19	1	2	3	4	6	7	9	10	12	1	2	3
21	1	3	3	5	7	8	9	11	12	1	3	4
23	2	4	4	6	7	9	10	12	1	2	4	5
25	3	5	5	7	8	10	11	12	2	3	5	6
27	4	6	6	8	9	11	12	1	3	4	6	7
29	5		7	9	10	11	1	2	4	5	7	8
31	6		8		11		1	3		6		9

1984

DATE	Ja	Fe	Mr	Ap	Ma	Jn	Jl	Ag	Se	Oc	Nv	De
1	9	11	12	1	2	4	5	7	9	10	11	12
3	10	12	12	2	3	5	6	8	10	11	12	1
5	11	12	1	3	4	6	7	9	10	11	1	2
7	12	1	2	4	5	7	8	10	11	12	2	3
9	1	2	3	5	6	8	9	10	12	1	2	3
11	1	3	4	5	7	9	10	11	1	2	3	5
13	2	4	5	6	8	9	11	12	2	3	4	6
15	3	5	6	7	9	10	11	1	2	4	5	6
17	4	6	7	8	10	11	12	2	3	4	6	7
19	5	7	8	9	10	12	1	2	4	5	7	8
21	6	8	9	10	11	1	2	3	5	6	8	9
23	7	9	9	11	12	1	3	4	6	7	9	10
25	8	10	10	12	1	2	4	5	6	8	10	11
27	9	10	11	1	2	3	4	6	7	9	11	12
29	10	11	12	1	3	4	5	7	8	10	12	1
31	11		1		3		6	8		11		1

For Further Exploration

Eleanor Bach, *Astrology from A to Z*. New York: Philosophical Library, 1990.

Dodie Edmands and Allan Edmands, *The Children's Astrologer*. New York: Hawthorn Books, 1978.

Roy A. Gallant, *Astrology: Sense or Nonsense?* Garden City, NY: Doubleday & Co., 1974.

Elizabeth S. Helfan, *Signs and Symbols of the Sun*. San Francisco: Seabury Press, 1974.

Brian Innes, Francis King, and Neil Powell, Fate and Fortune. New York: Crescent Books, 1989.

Gary Jennings, *The Teenager's Realistic Guide to Astrology*. New York: Association Press, 1971.

Troy Lawrence, *The Secret Message of the Zodiac*. San Bernardino, CA: Here's Life Publishers, Inc., 1990.

Llewellyn's 1991 Moon Sign Book. St. Paul, MN: Llewellyn, 1990. (New edition available each year.)

Llewellyn's Sun Sign Book: 1991 Horoscopes for Every Sign. St. Paul, MN: Llewellyn, 1990. (New edition available each year.)

Mary Orser, Rick Brightfield, and Glory Brightfield, *Instant Astrology*. New York: Harper Colophon Books, 1976.

J. Maya Pilkington and The Diagram Group, *Who Are You?* New York: Ballantine, 1986.

Bibliography

John Andenberg & John Weldon, *Astrology: Do the Heavens Rule Our Destiny?* Eugene, OR: Harvest House, 1989.

Douglas Bloch and Demetra George, *Astrology for Yourself.* Berkeley, CA: Wingbow Press, 1987.

Franklyn M. Branley, *Age of Aquarius: You and Astrology.* New York: Thomas Y. Crowell, 1979.

Nicholas Campion, *The Practical Astrologer.* New York: Harry N. Abrams, 1987.

Hilary M. Carey, "Astrology, Science, and Society," in *Astrology at the English Court in the Later Middle Ages*, ed. by Patrick Curry. Woodbridge, Suffolk, ENG: The Boydell Press, 1987.

Roger B. Culver and Philip A. Ianna, *Astrology: True or False? A Scientific Evaluation.* Buffalo, NY: Prometheus Books, 1988.

Roger B. Culver and Philip A. Ianna, *The Gemini Syndrome.* Buffalo, NY: Prometheus Books, 1984.

Ronald C. Davison, *Astrology: The Classic Guide to Understanding Your Horoscope.* Sebastopol, CA: CRCS Publications, 1987.

Dennis Elwell, *Cosmic Loom: The New Science of Astrology.* London: Unwin Hyman, 1987.

H. J. Eysenck and D. K. B. Nias, *Astrology: Science or Superstition?* New York: St. Martin's Press, 1982.

Sasha Fenton, *Rising Signs: The Astrological Guide to the Image We Project.* Wellingborough,

Northamptonshire, ENG: The Aquarian Press, 1989.

Leonard Everett Fisher, *Star Signs.* New York: Holiday House, 1983.

Bernard Fitzwalter, *The Complete Sun Sign Guide.* Wellingborough, Northamptonshire, ENG: The Aquarian Press, 1987.

Leslie Fleming-Mitchell, *Astrology Terms.* Philadelphia: Running Press, 1977.

Michel Gauquelin, *Written in the Stars.* Wellingborough, Northamptonshire, ENG: The Aquarian Press, 1988.

Fred Gettings, *The Arkana Dictionary of Astrology*, rev. ed. London: Arkana/Penguin, 1990.

Joseph F. Goodavage, *Write Your Own Horoscope*, rev. ed. New York: Signet, 1990.

Ernest A. Grant, *Tables of Midheavens and Ascendants.* Tempe, AZ: American Federation of Astrologers, 1954, 1987.

Liz Greene, *The Astrology of Fate.* York Beach, ME: Samuel Weiser, Inc., 1989.

Muriel Bruce Hasbrouck, *Tarot and Astrology: The Pursuit of Destiny.* Rochester, VT: Destiny Books, 1989.

Edith Hathaway, *Navigating by the Stars: Astrology and the Art of Decision-Making.* St. Paul, MN: Llewellyn, 1991.

Elinor Lander Horwitz, *The Soothsayer's Handbook: A Guide to Bad Signs and Good Vibrations.* New York: J.P. Lippincott, 1972.

Janis Huntley, *The Elements of Astrology.* Longmead, Shaftesbury, Dorset, ENG: Element Books, 1990.

Lawrence Jerome, *Astrology Disproved.* Buffalo, NY: Prometheus Books, 1977.

Marc Edmund Jones, *How to Learn Astrology.* Boulder, CO: Shambhala, 1969.

Richard Leigh, *Dreams and Illusions of Astrology.* Buffalo, NY: Prometheus Books, 1979.

Hugh MacCraig, *The Ephemeris of the Moon, 1800 to*

2000 Inclusive. Richmond, VA: Macoy Publishing Co., 1969.

Charlotte MacLeod, *Astrology for Skeptics*. New York: Macmillan, 1972.

Louis MacNeice, *Astrology*. Garden City, NY: Doubleday & Co., 1964.

Sondra Maie, *Fun Astrology*. New York: Julian Messner, 1981.

David Marks and Richard Kammann, *The Psychology of the Psychic*. Buffalo, NY: Prometheus Books, 1980.

Joan Negus, *Basic Astrology: A Guide for Teachers and Students*. San Diego: ACS Publications, 1990.

Alan Oken, *Alan Oken's Complete Astrology*, rev. ed. New York: Bantam, 1988.

Sydney Omarr, *Sydney Omarr's Astrology Guide for You in 1992*. New York: Signet, 1991. (New edition available each year.)

Derek Parker and Julia Parker, *The New Compleat Astrologer*. New York: Crown Publishers, Inc. 1984, 1990.

Robert Pelletier and Leonard Cataldo, *The Cosmic Informer: An Astrological Guide to Self-Discovery*. Boston: Little, Brown, & Co., 1984.

Beatrice Ryder, *Astrology: Your Personal Sun-Sign Guide*. New York: Bell Publishing Company/a division of Crown Publishers, Inc., 1969.

Frances Sakoian and Louis S. Acker, *The Astrologer's Handbook*. New York: Harper & Row, 1973.

Percy Seymour, *Astrology: The Evidence of Science*. London: Arkana/Penguin, 1990.

Charles R. Strohmer, *What Your Horoscope Doesn't Tell You*. Wheaton, IL: Tyndale, 1988.

John Anthony West, *The Case for Astrology*. London: Viking/Arkana, 1991.

Paul Wright, *Astrology in Action*. Sebastopol, CA: CRCS Publications, 1989.

Zolar, *The History of Astrology*. New York: Arco Publishing Co., 1972.

Index

About the Author

Mary-Paige Royer, a free-lance writer, lives in Minneapolis, Minnesota, with her husband and two children. She has been a professional writer for the past eight years and has written a variety of stories for local and national magazines. Topics have ranged from baby boomers and volunteerism, to passenger train travel, to improving memory. *Astrology: Opposing Viewpoints* is Royer's first book in the Great Mysteries series.

Picture Credits